AFFORDABLE
EATS

TASTE OF HOME BOOKS • RDA ENTHUSIAST BRANDS, LLC • MILWAUKEE, WI

Taste of Home

International Standard Book Number:
978-1-61765-824-2
LOCC: 2018951859
Component Number: 116700086H

Deputy Editor: Mark Hagen
Senior Art Director: Raeann Thompson
Senior Designer: Courtney Lovetere
Designer: Jazmin Delgado
Copy Editor: Ann Walter
Photographer: Grace Natoli Sheldon
Set Stylist: Dee Dee Jacq
Food Stylist: Kathryn Conrad

Pictured on front cover:
Cajun Chicken & Pasta, p. 37

Pictured on title page:
Sheet-Pan Pineapple Chicken Fajitas, p. 9

Pictured on back cover:
Sloppy Joes, p. 39;
Buffalo Chicken Biscuits, p. 98;
Blackened Pork Caesar Salad, p. 83;
Root Beer Float Pie, p. 105

Printed in USA
1 3 5 7 9 10 8 6 4 2

TABLE OF CONTENTS

GET SOCIAL WITH US

 LIKE US: facebook.com/tasteofhome | **PIN US:** pinterest.com/taste_of_home
 FOLLOW US: @tasteofhome | **TWEET US:** twitter.com/tasteofhome

TO FIND A RECIPE:
tasteofhome.com

TO SUBMIT A RECIPE:
tasteofhome.com/submit

TO FIND OUT ABOUT OTHER
TASTE OF HOME **PRODUCTS:**
shoptasteofhome.com

START SAVING MONEY TODAY!

Trim your grocery bill, beat the clock and surprise your family with the comforting favorites they crave. It's a snap with the 165 easy, economical and enticing recipes inside the new cookbook **Taste of Home Affordable Eats.**

From dinner classics and weeknight wonders to impressive desserts and swift snacks, these mouthwatering dishes keep flavor at a premium without taking bites out of your budget. Consider terrific entrees such as Stovetop Cheeseburger Pasta (p. 7), Sheet-Pan Pineapple Chicken Fajitas (p. 9) or even Grilled Brats with Sriracha Mayo (p. 14). These meals ring in at just $10 each.

You'll find bargain breakfasts and inexpensive lunch ideas that don't break the bank, as well as economical appetizers, incredible side dishes and no-fuss recipes for tasty extras that round out menus and beat grocery budgets. Save money and savor sensational foods today. It's easy with **Affordable Eats** at your fingertips!

SAVE TIME, TOO!

Look for these icons when you need dinner fast—while keeping money in your wallet:

FAST FIX These sensational recipes come together in 30 minutes or less.

5 INGREDIENTS With the exception of water, salt, pepper, oils and optional ingredients, these dishes call for only a handful of items.

SLOW COOKER Come out ahead when you let your slow cooker do the work.

BIG SAVINGS START WITH A LITTLE PLANNING

Tired of pinching pennies? Become a smarter shopper when you brush up on these easy ideas for slashing your grocery bills.

Start by creating a weekly or monthly food budget. Allocating a certain amount of money for grocery expenses instantly sets you up for success because you're more likely to seek out sales and less likely to make impulse purchases.

Once your budget is set, plan to shop no more than once per week. After all, the fewer times you hit the store, the more you'll save—on time and gas, as well as money. Buying groceries once a week also gets you into the cost-saving habit of planning meals for a week, versus ordering pizza, hitting a drive-thru or returning to the store for additional groceries.

Before shopping, take inventory of your fridge, freezer and pantry. Make a shopping list of what you need and take note of what you don't need. When you're at the store, you won't impulse-buy an item you already have. Once your grocery list is made, clip applicable coupons. Be sure to only clip coupons for the items on your shopping list.

In fact, make coupons your new best friends. Pick up a copy of the Sunday paper each week and start clipping, or hit the internet and take advantage of online coupons. Don't forget to make the most of your grocer's weekly specials and membership programs.

When it is time to shop, make sure you have your shopping list, coupons, membership card and a full stomach. You've heard it before, but it bears repeating: Don't go grocery shopping on an empty stomach. The temptation to buy things not on your list can be too great for a hungry shopper to avoid. That's it! Now it's time to visit the supermarket with confidence...and check out with extra cash in your wallet.

QUICKPEA CURRY

MEALS FOR $10 OR LESS

It's true! You can save money, get out of the kitchen quickly and serve your family mouthwatering dinners. The following entrees ring up at just $10 (or less) and are guaranteed to rise to the top of your list of favorites.

QUICKPEA CURRY

This colorful curry is a nice change of pace any night of the week. I usually have most of the ingredients on hand, but I substitute fresh peas for frozen when in season.
—*Beth Fleming, Downers Grove, IL*

PREP: 15 min. • **COOK:** 35 min.
MAKES: 6 servings

- 1 Tbsp. canola oil
- 1 medium onion, finely chopped
- 2 garlic cloves, minced
- 1 Tbsp. curry powder
- 2 cans (14½ oz. each) diced tomatoes, undrained
- 2 cans (15 oz. each) chickpeas or garbanzo beans, rinsed and drained
- 2 cups cubed peeled sweet potato (about 1 medium)
- 1 cup light coconut milk
- 2 tsp. sugar
- ¼ tsp. crushed red pepper flakes
- 1 cup uncooked whole wheat pearl (Israeli) couscous
- 1½ cups frozen peas (about 6 oz.)
- ¼ tsp. salt
   Chopped fresh parsley
   Plain yogurt, optional

1. In a large skillet, heat the oil over medium heat; saute the onion and garlic with curry powder until tender, 3-4 minutes. Stir in the tomatoes, chickpeas, sweet potato, coconut milk, sugar and pepper flakes; bring to a boil. Reduce heat; simmer, uncovered, until the mixture is thickened and the sweet potato is tender, 25-30 minutes, stirring occasionally.
2. Meanwhile, prepare couscous and peas separately according to package directions. Stir salt into peas.
3. To serve, divide the couscous among six bowls. Top with the chickpea mixture, peas, parsley and, if desired, yogurt.
1 SERVING: 390 cal., 8g fat (2g sat. fat), 0 chol., 561mg sod., 68g carb. (14g sugars, 13g fiber), 13g pro.

OUR TWO CENT$
Save money by freezing any leftover coconut milk, or refrigerate the extra milk and stir it into the next morning's oatmeal or coffee. You can even add it to whisked eggs before scrambling.

STOVETOP
CHEESEBURGER
PASTA

FAST FIX
STOVETOP CHEESEBURGER PASTA

Cheeseburgers are delicious in any form, but I'm partial to this creamy pasta dish that seriously tastes just like the real thing. It's weeknight comfort in a bowl.
—*Tracy Avis, Peterborough, ON*

TAKES: 30 min. • **MAKES:** 8 servings

- 1 pkg. (16 oz.) penne pasta
- 1 lb. ground beef
- ¼ cup butter, cubed
- ½ cup all-purpose flour
- 2 cups 2% milk
- 1¼ cups beef broth
- 1 Tbsp. Worcestershire sauce
- 3 tsp. ground mustard
- 2 cans (14½ oz. each) diced tomatoes, drained
- 4 green onions, chopped
- 3 cups shredded Colby-Monterey Jack cheese, divided
- ⅔ cup grated Parmesan cheese, divided

1. Cook the pasta according to package directions; drain.
2. Meanwhile, in a Dutch oven, cook and crumble the beef over medium heat until no longer pink, 5-7 minutes. Remove from the pan with a slotted spoon; pour off the drippings.
3. In same pan, melt butter over low heat; stir in the flour until smooth. Cook and stir until lightly browned, 2-3 minutes (do not burn). Gradually whisk in the milk, broth, Worcestershire sauce and mustard. Bring to a boil, stirring constantly; cook and stir until thickened, 1-2 minutes. Stir in the tomatoes; return to a boil. Reduce the heat; simmer, covered, 5 minutes.
4. Stir in green onions, pasta and beef; heat through. Stir in half of the cheeses until melted. Sprinkle with the remaining cheese; remove from heat. Let stand, covered, until the cheese is melted.
1½ CUPS: 616 cals, 29g fat (17g sat. fat), 98mg chol., 727mg sod., 56g carb. (7g sugars, 3g fiber), 33g pro.

SHEET-PAN PINEAPPLE
CHICKEN FAJITAS

SHEET-PAN PINEAPPLE CHICKEN FAJITAS

I combined chicken and pineapple for a different flavor in our fajitas. These are a bit on the sweet side but my family loves them!
—Nancy Heishman, Las Vegas, NV

- -

PREP: 20 min. • **COOK:** 20 min.
MAKES: 6 servings

- 2 Tbsp. coconut oil, melted
- 3 tsp. chili powder
- 2 tsp. ground cumin
- 1 tsp. garlic powder
- ¾ tsp. kosher salt
- 1½ lbs. chicken tenderloins, halved lengthwise
- 1 large red or sweet onion, halved and sliced (about 2 cups)
- 1 large sweet red pepper, cut into ½-in. strips
- 1 large green pepper, cut into ½-in. strips
- 1 Tbsp. minced seeded jalapeno pepper
- 2 cans (8 oz. each) unsweetened pineapple tidbits, drained
- 2 Tbsp. honey
- 2 Tbsp. lime juice
- 12 corn tortillas (6 in.), warmed
  Optional toppings: pico de gallo, sour cream, shredded Mexican cheese blend and sliced avocado
  Lime wedges, optional

1. Preheat oven to 425°. In a large bowl, mix first five ingredients; stir in chicken. Add the onion, peppers, pineapple, honey and lime juice; toss to combine. Spread evenly in two greased 15x10x1-in. baking pans.
2. Roast 10 minutes, rotating pans halfway through cooking. Remove pans from oven; preheat broiler.
3. Broil chicken mixture, one pan at a time, 3-4 in. from heat until vegetables are lightly browned and the chicken is no longer pink, 3-5 minutes. Serve in tortillas, with toppings and lime wedges as desired.

2 FAJITAS: 359 cal., 8g fat (4g sat. fat), 56mg chol., 372mg sod., 45g carb. (19g sugars, 6g fiber), 31g pro. **DIABETIC EXCHANGES:** 3 starch, 3 lean meat, 1 fat.

PRESSURE-COOKER BEEF TIPS

AMY LENTS
Grant Forks, ND

PRESSURE-COOKER BEEF TIPS

These beef tips remind me of a favorite childhood meal. I like to cook them with mushrooms and serve over brown rice, noodles or leftover mashed potatoes.
—Amy Lents, Grand Forks, ND

- -

PREP: 20 min. • **COOK:** 15 min.
MAKES: 4 servings

- 3 tsp. olive oil
- 1 beef top sirloin steak (1 lb.), cubed
- ½ tsp. salt
- ¼ tsp. pepper
- ⅓ cup dry red wine or beef broth
- ½ lb. sliced baby portobello mushrooms
- 1 small onion, halved and sliced
- 2 cups beef broth
- 1 Tbsp. Worcestershire sauce
- 3 to 4 Tbsp. cornstarch
- ¼ cup cold water
  Hot cooked mashed potatoes

1. Select saute setting on a 6-qt. electric pressure cooker and adjust for high heat. Add 2 tsp. oil. Sprinkle beef with salt and pepper. Brown meat in batches, adding oil as needed. Transfer meat to a bowl. Add wine to cooker, stirring to loosen browned bits. Return beef to cooker; add the mushrooms, onion, broth and Worcestershire sauce. Lock lid; make sure vent is closed. Select manual setting; adjust pressure to high and set time for 15 minutes. When finished cooking, quick-release pressure according to the manufacturer's directions.
2. Select saute setting and adjust for high heat; bring liquid to a boil. In a small bowl, mix the cornstarch and water until smooth; gradually stir into beef mixture. Cook and stir until sauce is thickened, 1-2 minutes. Serve with mashed potatoes.

1 CUP: 212 cal., 7g fat (2g sat. fat), 46mg chol., 836mg sod., 8g carb. (2g sugars, 1g fiber), 27g pro. **DIABETIC EXCHANGES:** 3 lean meat, ½ starch, ½ fat.

OUR TWO CENT$

The next day, stir a little heavy cream or sour cream into the leftover sauce and meat mixture. Reheat and serve over pasta for another meal.

FAST FIX
CURRIED CHICKEN SKILLET

This protein-packed, 30-minute skillet dish is loaded with bright flavor. A little curry and fresh ginger really make the veggies, chicken and quinoa pop.
—*Ruth Hartunian-Alumbaugh, Willimantic, CT*

- -

TAKES: 30 min. • **MAKES:** 4 servings

1⅓ cups plus ½ cup reduced-sodium chicken broth, divided
⅔ cup quinoa, rinsed
1 Tbsp. canola oil
1 medium sweet potato, diced
1 medium onion, chopped
1 celery rib, chopped
1 cup frozen peas
2 garlic cloves, minced
1 tsp. minced fresh gingerroot
3 tsp. curry powder
¼ tsp. salt
2 cups shredded cooked chicken

1. In a small saucepan, bring 1⅓ cups broth to a boil. Add the quinoa. Reduce the heat; simmer, covered, until liquid is absorbed, 12-15 minutes.
2. In a large skillet, heat oil over medium-high heat; saute sweet potato, onion and celery until potato is tender, 10-12 minutes. Add peas, garlic, ginger and seasonings; cook and stir 2 minutes. Stir in chicken and remaining broth; heat through. Stir in quinoa.
2 CUPS: 367 cal., 11g fat (2g sat. fat), 62mg chol., 450mg sod., 39g carb. (8g sugars, 6g fiber), 29g pro. **DIABETIC EXCHANGES:** 3 lean meat, 2½ starch, ½ fat.

SAUCY CHICKEN & TORTELLINI

This heartwarming dish is something I threw together years ago for my oldest daughter. When she's having a rough day, I put on the slow cooker and prepare this special recipe.
—*Mary Morgan, Dallas, TX*

- -

PREP: 10 min. • **COOK:** 6¼ hours
MAKES: 8 servings

1½ lbs. boneless skinless chicken breasts, cut into 1-in. cubes
½ lb. sliced fresh mushrooms
1 large onion, chopped
1 medium sweet red pepper, cut into ½-in. pieces
1 medium green pepper, cut into ½-in. pieces
1 can (2¼ oz.) sliced ripe olives, drained
1 jar (24 oz.) marinara sauce
1 jar (15 oz.) Alfredo sauce
2 pkg. (9 oz. each) refrigerated cheese tortellini
    Grated Parmesan cheese, optional
    Torn fresh basil, optional

1. In a 5-qt. slow cooker, combine first seven ingredients. Cook, covered, on low until the chicken is tender, 6-8 hours.
2. Stir in the Alfredo sauce and the tortellini. Cook, covered, until the tortellini is tender, 15-20 minutes. If desired, top with Parmesan cheese and basil.
FREEZE OPTION: Freeze cooled, cooked mixture in freezer containers. To use, partially thaw in refrigerator overnight. Microwave, covered, on high, in a microwave-safe dish until heated through, stirring gently and adding a little water if necessary.
1¼ CUPS: 437 cal., 15g fat (7g sat. fat), 91mg chol., 922mg sod., 44g carb. (8g sugars, 5g fiber), 31g pro.

SAUCY CHICKEN & TORTELLINI

QUICK SESAME
CHICKEN NOODLES

QUICK SESAME CHICKEN NOODLES

I really enjoy experimenting with different ingredients and spices in my stir-fry recipes. As my children get older, I have many more evenings when I need to whip up dinner quickly, and this dish with chicken strips and ramen noodles fits the bill deliciously.
—*Heather Chambers, Largo, FL*

- -

TAKES: 25 min. • **MAKES:** 4 servings

- 1 Tbsp. sesame oil
- 1 pkg. (22 oz.) frozen grilled chicken breast strips
- 1 medium yellow summer squash, thinly sliced
- 1 cup julienned carrots
- ⅓ cup halved fresh snow peas
- 3 garlic cloves, minced
- 2 pkg. (3 oz. each) chicken ramen noodles, broken into small pieces
- 1⅓ cups water
- ⅓ cup white wine or chicken broth
- 3 Tbsp. reduced-sodium teriyaki sauce
- 4 green onions, sliced

1. In a large skillet, heat oil over medium-high heat; saute the chicken, squash and carrots until chicken is heated through, 6-8 minutes. Add the snow peas; cook until vegetables are crisp-tender, 3-4 minutes. Add the garlic and the contents of one ramen seasoning packet (discard or save second packet for another use); cook and stir 1 minute.
2. Add noodles, water, wine and teriyaki sauce. Bring to a boil; cook, uncovered, until the noodles are tender, 3-4 minutes, stirring occasionally.
3. Remove from heat; stir in green onions. Serve immediately.
1½ CUPS: 460 cal., 15g fat (5g sat. fat), 93mg chol., 1626mg sod., 37g carb. (6g sugars, 3g fiber), 45g pro.

OUR TWO CENT$

The ramen noodles soak up the sauce to become extra flavorful. This recipe is perfect for using up leftovers. Try it with pork or rotisserie chicken.

HEALTHIER-THAN-EGG ROLLS

Frying anything at home can be a little intimidating for me, but I love egg rolls. With this recipe, I've figured out a way to get the best part without the mess. This can be used to stuff egg roll wrappers, but we love it on its own, too.
—*Sue Mitchell, Kerrville, TX*

- -

TAKES: 25 min. • **MAKES:** 4 servings

- 1 lb. lean ground chicken
- 1½ cups sliced fresh mushrooms
- 1 medium onion, chopped
- 2 garlic cloves, minced
- 1 tsp. minced fresh gingerroot
- 2 Tbsp. reduced-sodium soy sauce
- 1 pkg. (14 oz.) coleslaw mix
- 1 Tbsp. sesame oil
- 3 cups hot cooked brown rice
- ½ cup sweet-and-sour sauce
  Wonton strips, optional

1. In a large skillet, cook and crumble chicken with mushrooms, onion, garlic and ginger over medium-high heat until no longer pink, 6-8 minutes; drain. Stir in soy sauce.
2. Add the coleslaw mix; cook and stir until wilted, 3-4 minutes. Stir in sesame oil. Serve with the rice and sweet-and-sour sauce. If desired, top with wonton strips.
1¼ CUPS CHICKEN MIXTURE WITH ¾ CUP RICE: 451 cal., 11g fat (3g sat. fat), 81mg chol., 591mg sod., 58g carb. (13g sugars, 6g fiber), 30g pro.

PAPRIKA CHICKEN
STROGANOFF

and mustard; bring to a boil. Cook, uncovered, until liquid is reduced by half, 10-12 minutes. Stir in the chicken; cook, uncovered, over medium-low until chicken is no longer pink, 3-5 minutes.

5. Stir in creme fraiche, parsley and the remaining salt and pepper; remove from heat. Stir in noodles.

1⅔ CUPS: 505 cal., 24g fat (12g sat. fat), 133mg chol., 874mg sod., 35g carb. (4g sugars, 3g fiber), 33g pro.

FAST FIX | 5 INGREDIENTS

CRISPY DILL TILAPIA

Every week I try to serve a new healthy fish. This dish of economical tilapia is always a winner with its delicious fresh dill and panko bread crumb crust.
—*Tamara Huron, New Market, AL*

- -

TAKES: 20 min. • **MAKES:** 4 servings

- 1 cup panko (Japanese) bread crumbs
- 2 Tbsp. olive oil
- 2 Tbsp. snipped fresh dill
- ¼ tsp. salt
- ⅛ tsp. pepper
- 4 tilapia fillets (6 oz. each)
- 1 Tbsp. lemon juice
  Lemon wedges

1. Preheat oven to 400°. Toss together the first five ingredients.
2. Place the tilapia in a 15x10x1-in. baking pan coated with cooking spray; brush with lemon juice. Top with the crumb mixture, patting to help adhere.
3. Bake, uncovered, on an upper oven rack until the fish fillets just begin to flake easily with a fork, 12-15 minutes. Serve with the lemon wedges.

1 FILLET: 256 cal., 9g fat (2g sat. fat), 83mg chol., 251mg sod., 10g carb. (1g sugars, 1g fiber), 34g pro. **DIABETIC EXCHANGES:** 5 lean meat, 1½ fat, ½ starch.

PAPRIKA CHICKEN STROGANOFF

Stroganoff is a favorite comfort food of mine. While it is traditionally a beef dish, it can easily be adapted for other proteins, and it is just as delicious. I am consuming less red meat lately, so I created this creamy chicken stroganoff. Now I get to enjoy the comforting sauce with the added benefits of a lighter white meat.
—*Leo Lo, Norfolk, VA*

- -

PREP: 20 min. • **COOK:** 30 min.
MAKES: 6 servings

- 8 oz. uncooked wide egg noodles
- 1½ lbs. boneless skinless chicken breasts, cut into ½-in.-wide strips
- 2 tsp. paprika
- 1½ tsp. salt, divided
- ¾ tsp. pepper, divided
- 1 Tbsp. olive oil
- 1 lb. sliced baby portobello mushrooms
- 1 Tbsp. butter
- 1 large red onion, halved and sliced
- 3 garlic cloves, minced
- 1 cup dry white wine or chicken stock
- 1 cup chicken stock
- 1 Tbsp. Worcestershire sauce
- 1 Tbsp. Dijon mustard
- 1 cup creme fraiche or sour cream
- 1 Tbsp. minced fresh Italian parsley

1. Cook the noodles according to package directions; drain.
2. Meanwhile, toss chicken with paprika, ½ tsp. salt and ¼ tsp. pepper. In a Dutch oven, heat the oil over medium-high heat. In batches, saute chicken until browned, 2-3 minutes. Remove from pan.
3. In same pan, saute mushrooms in butter until lightly browned, 4-5 minutes. Add the onion; cook and stir 3-4 minutes or until softened. Add garlic; cook and stir 1 minute.
4. Add wine, stirring to loosen browned bits from pan. Add stock, Worcestershire sauce

---

OUR TWO CENT$
This easy breading would complement most types of fish. Try it on salmon if you prefer. If you don't have fresh dill, a bit of fresh thyme would be great with fish and lemon. Tossing the bread crumbs with a bit of oil helps it crisp up in the short amount of time it takes to cook the fish.

**CRISPY DILL
TILAPIA**

FAST FIX
GRILLED BRATS WITH SRIRACHA MAYO

I am a Sriracha fanatic, so that's what inspired this dish. You can boil the brats in your favorite beer to add even more flavor before grilling. I like to spread a bit of garlic butter on lightly toasted buns, too.
—*Quincie Ball, Olympia, WA*

- -

TAKES: 20 min. • **MAKES:** 4 servings

½ cup mayonnaise
⅓ cup minced roasted
   sweet red peppers
3 Tbsp. Sriracha Asian hot chili sauce
1 tsp. hot pepper sauce
4 fully cooked bratwurst links
4 brat buns or hot dog buns, split
½ cup dill pickle relish
½ cup finely chopped red onion
   Ketchup, optional

Mix first four ingredients. Grill bratwursts, covered, over medium-low heat until browned and heated through, 7-10 minutes, turning occasionally. Serve in the buns with the mayonnaise mixture, relish, onion and, if desired, ketchup.

1 SERVING: 742 cal., 49g fat (13g sat. fat), 65mg chol., 2020mg sod., 54g carb. (10g sugars, 2g fiber), 20g pro.

HEALTH TIP: Sodium loves company in these brats—sausage, bread and condiments are all on the high-sodium list. Cut back by skipping the relish and using half of the sweet-spicy sauce. You'll save more than 600 milligrams per serving.

ROXANNE CHAN
Albany, CA

FAST FIX
SPAGHETTI & MEATBALL SKILLET SUPPER

I developed this one-skillet spaghetti and meatball dish to cut down on cooking time for busy nights. The beans, artichokes and tomatoes bump up the nutrition factor, while the lemon and parsley make it pop with brightness.
—*Roxanne Chan, Albany, CA*

- -

TAKES: 30 min. • **MAKES:** 6 servings

12 oz. frozen fully cooked
    Italian turkey meatballs
1 Tbsp. olive oil
1 can (28 oz.) whole tomatoes,
   undrained, broken up
1 can (15 oz.) cannellini beans,
   rinsed and drained
1 can (14 oz.) water-packed quartered
   artichoke hearts, drained
½ tsp. Italian seasoning
1 can (14½ oz.) reduced-
   sodium chicken broth
4 oz. uncooked spaghetti, broken
   into 2-in. pieces (about 1⅓ cups)
¼ cup chopped fresh parsley
1 Tbsp. lemon juice
   Grated Parmesan cheese

1. Prepare meatballs according to package directions. In a large skillet, heat the oil over medium heat; add meatballs and cook until browned slightly, turning occasionally.
2. Add tomatoes, beans, artichoke hearts, Italian seasoning and broth; bring to a boil. Stir in the spaghetti; return to a boil. Reduce heat; simmer, covered, until the spaghetti is tender, 10-12 minutes, stirring occasionally.
3. Stir in the parsley and lemon juice. Serve with Parmesan cheese.

1⅓ CUPS: 330 cal., 10g fat (2g sat. fat), 43mg chol., 1051mg sod., 38g carb. (5g sugars, 6g fiber), 20g pro.

CHILI-LIME MUSHROOM TACOS

I used to make this dish with beef, but substituting with portobello mushrooms turned it into my family's vegetarian favorite. It's quick, nutritious, low-fat, economical and tasty.
—*Greg Fontenot, The Woodlands, TX*

TAKES: 25 min. • **MAKES:** 4 servings

- 4 large portobello mushrooms (about ¾ lb.)
- 1 Tbsp. olive oil
- 1 medium sweet red pepper, cut into strips
- 1 medium onion, halved and thinly sliced
- 2 garlic cloves, minced
- 1½ tsp. chili powder
- ½ tsp. salt
- ½ tsp. ground cumin
- ¼ tsp. crushed red pepper flakes
- 1 tsp. grated lime zest
- 2 Tbsp. lime juice
- 8 corn tortillas (6 in.), warmed
- 1 cup shredded pepper jack cheese

1. Remove stems from the mushrooms; if desired, remove the gills using a spoon. Cut mushroom caps into ½-in. slices.
2. In a large skillet, heat oil over medium-high heat; saute the mushrooms, red pepper strips and onion until mushrooms are tender, 5-7 minutes. Stir in garlic, seasonings, lime zest and juice; cook and stir 1 minute. Serve in tortillas; top with cheese.

2 TACOS: 300 cal., 14g fat (6g sat. fat), 30mg chol., 524mg sod., 33g carb. (5g sugars, 6g fiber), 13g pro. **DIABETIC EXCHANGES:** 2 vegetable, 1½ starch, 1 medium-fat meat, ½ fat.

HEALTH TIP: Making these same tacos with lean ground beef adds almost 4 g. saturated fat per serving. That's a good reason for a meatless Taco Tuesday!

CHICKEN CORDON BLEU SKILLET

Here's a good and hearty supper. If I have fresh mushrooms on hand, I slice them and toss them in the skillet. You could also add leftover cooked vegetables such as broccoli or cauliflower.
—*Sandy Harz, Spring Lake, MI*

TAKES: 25 min. • **MAKES:** 4 servings

- 8 oz. uncooked medium egg noodles (about 5 cups)
- 1 lb. boneless skinless chicken breasts, cut in 1-in. pieces
- ½ tsp. pepper
- 1 Tbsp. butter
- 1 can (10¾ oz.) condensed cream of chicken soup, undiluted
- ½ cup shredded Swiss cheese
- ½ cup cubed fully cooked ham
- ¼ cup water
  Minced fresh parsley

1. Cook noodles according to the package directions; drain.
2. Meanwhile, sprinkle chicken with pepper. In a large skillet, heat butter over medium-high heat; saute chicken just until browned, 3-5 minutes. Stir in soup, cheese, ham and water; cook, covered, over medium heat until the cheese is melted and the chicken is no longer pink, 6-8 minutes, stirring occasionally. Stir in the noodles. Sprinkle with parsley.

1½ CUPS: 516 cal., 18g fat (8g sat. fat), 147mg chol., 878mg sod., 47g carb. (2g sugars, 3g fiber), 40g pro.

CHILI-LIME
MUSHROOM
TACOS

CHICKEN
& WAFFLES

BREAKFAST ON A BUDGET

Rising and shining doesn't have to mean breaking the bank. Kick-start the day with these finger-licking recipes that keep flavor at a premium and cost to a minimum. From grab-and-go breakfast sandwiches to special Sunday brunch items and coffeehouse copycats, these affordable ideas will rise to the top of your early-morning mainstays.

CHICKEN & WAFFLES

My first experience with chicken and waffles sent my taste buds into orbit. I originally made the dish as an appetizer, but we all love this idea as an eye-opening entree, too.
—*Lisa Renshaw, Kansas City, MO*

- -

TAKES: 25 min. • **MAKES:** 4 servings

- 12 **frozen crispy chicken strips (about 18 oz.)**
- ½ **cup honey**
- 2 **tsp. hot pepper sauce**
- 8 **frozen waffles, toasted**

1. Bake chicken strips according to package directions. Meanwhile, in a small bowl, mix honey and pepper sauce.
2. Cut chicken into bite-sized pieces; serve on waffles. Drizzle with honey mixture.
1 SERVING: 643 cal., 22g fat (3g sat. fat), 32mg chol., 958mg sod., 93g carb. (39g sugars, 6g fiber), 21g pro.

RICH HAZELNUT COFFEE

I love trying new recipes and entertaining friends and relatives. This beverage couldn't be more perfect for doing just that. Coffee lovers, your favorite sipper just got better!
—*Sharon Delaney-Chronis, South Milwaukee, WI*

- -

TAKES: 15 min. • **MAKES:** 4 servings

- 3 **cups hot brewed coffee**
- ½ **cup packed brown sugar**
- 2 **Tbsp. butter**
- ¾ **cup half-and-half cream**
- ¼ **tsp. almond extract**
  Whipped cream and instant espresso powder, optional

1. In a large saucepan, combine the coffee, brown sugar and butter. Cook and stir over medium heat until sugar is dissolved. Stir in cream; heat through.
2. Remove from the heat; stir in extract. Ladle into mugs. Garnish with the whipped cream and dust with the espresso powder if desired.
1 CUP: 383 cal., 10g fat (7g sat. fat), 38mg chol., 80mg sod., 49g carb. (47g sugars, 0 fiber), 2g pro.

BRATWURST HASH

BRATWURST HASH

The next time you make brats, try skipping the buns. This colorful hash is a fast skillet meal that really sticks to your ribs.
—*Marie Parker, Milwaukee, WI*

- -

TAKES: 30 min. • **MAKES:** 4 servings

- 4 **uncooked bratwurst links, casings removed**
- 1 **medium green pepper, chopped**
- 1 **pkg. (20 oz.) refrigerated diced potatoes with onion**
- 1 **cup fresh or frozen corn, thawed**
- ¼ **cup chopped roasted sweet red pepper**
- ¼ **tsp. salt or ½ tsp. seasoned salt**
- ¾ **cup shredded Colby-Monterey Jack cheese**

1. In a large nonstick skillet, cook bratwurst and green pepper over medium heat just until sausage is no longer pink, 4-6 minutes, breaking up sausage into large crumbles.
2. Stir in potatoes, corn, red pepper and salt; spread evenly onto bottom of skillet. Cook 10 minutes without stirring. Turn mixture over; cook until the potatoes are tender, 7-8 minutes longer. Sprinkle with cheese.
1½ CUPS: 506 cal., 31g fat (13g sat. fat), 82mg chol., 1458mg sod., 35g carb. (3g sugars, 3g fiber), 19g pro.

TWICE-BAKED BREAKFAST POTATOES FOR TWO

A leftover baked potato was the inspiration for this impromptu meal. The combo of crispy bacon and savory sausage makes it a hearty breakfast dish as well as a filling lunch or even dinner.
—*William Brock, Amelia, OH*

- -

PREP: 30 min. • **BAKE:** 15 min.
MAKES: 2 servings

- 1 large baking potato
- ¾ tsp. butter
- 1 large egg, beaten
- 3 oz. bulk pork sausage
- 1 Tbsp. sour cream
- 2 bacon strips, cooked and crumbled
- 3 Tbsp. shredded cheddar cheese, divided
- 2 Tbsp. minced chives, divided
- ¾ tsp. minced fresh parsley
- ⅛ tsp. salt
- ⅛ tsp. pepper
  Additional sour cream, optional

1. Scrub and pierce the potato; place on a microwave-safe plate. Microwave potato, uncovered, on high until tender, turning once, 15-17 minutes.

2. Meanwhile, in a large skillet, melt butter over medium-high heat. Add the egg; cook and stir until set. Remove and set aside. In the same skillet, cook sausage over medium heat until no longer pink; drain and set aside.

3. When potato is cool enough to handle, cut in half lengthwise. Scoop out the pulp, leaving thin shells. In a large bowl, mash the pulp with sour cream. Stir in bacon, 2 Tbsp. cheese, 1 Tbsp. chives, parsley, salt, pepper, egg and sausage. Spoon into potato shells.

4. Place on a baking sheet. Bake, uncovered, at 375° until heated through, 12-15 minutes. Sprinkle with the remaining cheese and chives. Serve with additional sour cream if desired.

1 STUFFED POTATO HALF: 375 cal., 19g fat (9g sat. fat), 149mg chol., 590mg sod., 35g carb. (4g sugars, 3g fiber), 15g pro.

CRANBERRY ORANGE PANCAKES

CRANBERRY ORANGE PANCAKES

Perfect for a special morning meal, these fluffy pancakes are drop-dead gorgeous. Best of all, they're ready in minutes and brimming with sweet, tart and tangy flavor. Seconds, anyone?
—*Nancy Zimmerman,*
Cape May Court House, NJ

- -

PREP: 20 min. • **COOK:** 5 min./batch
MAKES: 12 pancakes (1¼ cups syrup)

SYRUP
- 1 cup fresh or frozen cranberries
- ⅔ cup orange juice
- ½ cup sugar
- 3 Tbsp. maple syrup

PANCAKES
- 2 cups biscuit/baking mix
- 2 Tbsp. sugar
- 2 tsp. baking powder
- 2 large eggs
- 1 large egg yolk
- 1 cup evaporated milk
- 2 Tbsp. orange juice
- 1 tsp. grated orange zest
- ½ cup chopped fresh or frozen cranberries
  Orange zest strips, optional

1. In a small saucepan, bring the cranberries, orange juice and sugar to a boil. Reduce the heat; simmer, uncovered, for 5 minutes. Cool slightly. With a slotted spoon, remove ¼ cup cranberries; set aside.

2. In a blender, process cranberry mixture until smooth. Transfer to a small bowl; stir in the maple syrup and reserved cranberries.

3. In a large bowl, combine the biscuit mix, sugar and baking powder. In another bowl, whisk the eggs, egg yolk, milk, orange juice and zest. Stir into dry ingredients just until blended. Fold in chopped cranberries.

4. Drop batter by ¼ cupfuls onto a greased hot griddle; turn when bubbles form on top. Cook until second side is golden brown. Serve with syrup. Garnish with orange zest strips if desired.

3 PANCAKES WITH ⅓ CUP SYRUP:
574 cal., 17g fat (7g sat. fat), 177mg chol., 1055mg sod., 94g carb. (53g sugars, 3g fiber), 12g pro.

APPLE CINNAMON OMELET

This sweet and savory omelet is a cinch to whip up and costs next to nothing! The yummy apple-cinnamon filling is a delightful change of pace from the cheese or ham omelets everyone is used to.
—*Agnes Ward, Stratford, ON*

- -

TAKES: 20 min. • **MAKES:** 1 serving

½	cup thinly sliced peeled tart apple
2	tsp. sugar
¼	tsp. ground cinnamon
2	Tbsp. butter, divided
3	large eggs
3	Tbsp. water
⅛	tsp. salt
⅛	tsp. pepper
	Sweetened whipped cream

1. In a small nonstick skillet, saute the apple, sugar and cinnamon in 1 Tbsp. butter. Remove from skillet and set aside.
2. In the same skillet, melt remaining butter over medium-high heat. Whisk eggs, water, salt and pepper. Add egg mixture to skillet (mixture should set immediately at edges).
3. As eggs set, push cooked edges toward the center, letting uncooked portion flow underneath. When the eggs are set, spoon apple mixture on one side; fold other side over filling. Slide omelet onto a plate. Serve with whipped cream.
1 OMELET: 476 cal., 38g fat (19g sat. fat), 695mg chol., 667mg sod., 17g carb. (15g sugars, 1g fiber), 19g pro.

OUR TWO CENT$
Although apples are available all year long, each variety has its own peak season. Always select apples that are firm and have a smooth, unblemished skin that is free from bruises. Store unwashed apples in the refrigerator away from other vegetables with strong aromas. Apples can be refrigerated for up to 6 weeks.

BREAKFAST TORTAS

CAROLYN KUMPE
El Dorado, CA

BREAKFAST TORTAS

My husband likes these rolls served with pickled jalapenos. Save more money when you substitute leftover taco meat, grilled steak or cooked chicken for the bacon.
—*Carolyn Kumpe, El Dorado, CA*

- -

PREP: 25 min. • **BAKE:** 15 min.
MAKES: 4 servings

4	ciabatta rolls
¾	cup refried black beans
⅓	cup sour cream
¼	cup minced fresh cilantro
2	tsp. lime juice
3	to 5 drops chipotle hot pepper sauce
⅛	tsp. salt
4	large eggs
½	cup shredded Monterey Jack cheese
1	tsp. olive oil
4	cooked bacon strips, halved
½	medium ripe avocado, peeled and sliced
½	cup salsa
2	green onions, chopped

1. Cut the top third off each roll; hollow out the bottom, leaving a ½-in. shell (discard removed bread or save for another use). Place the roll bottoms on an ungreased baking sheet.
2. In a small bowl, combine the beans, sour cream, cilantro, lime juice, chipotle pepper sauce and salt. Spread ¼ cup inside each roll. Carefully break an egg into each roll. Bake at 400° for 10 minutes.
3. Sprinkle cheese over eggs. Brush roll tops with olive oil; place on the baking sheet. Bake until the egg whites are completely set and the yolks begin to thicken but are not firm, 5-8 minutes longer. Top each with bacon, avocado, salsa and onions. Replace roll tops.
1 TORTA: 677 cal., 24g fat (8g sat. fat), 244mg chol., 1279mg sod., 94g carb. (8g sugars, 8g fiber), 28g pro.

DROP BISCUITS & GRAVY

We enjoy these flaky biscuits covered with creamy gravy not only for breakfast, but sometimes for dinner, too!
—*Darlene Brenden, Salem, OR*

- -

TAKES: 20 min. • **MAKES:** 4 servings

- 1 cup all-purpose flour
- 1½ tsp. baking powder
- ⅛ tsp. salt
- ½ cup 2% milk
- 2 Tbsp. butter, melted

GRAVY

- ½ lb. bulk pork sausage
- 1 Tbsp. butter
- 3 Tbsp. all-purpose flour
- 1¾ cups 2% milk
- ⅛ tsp. salt
- ½ tsp. pepper

1. Preheat oven to 450°. Whisk together the flour, baking powder and salt. In another bowl, whisk together the milk and butter; stir into dry ingredients just until blended. Divide dough into four portions and drop onto a parchment paper-lined baking sheet; bake until golden brown, 10-12 minutes.

2. In a small saucepan, cook and crumble sausage over medium heat until no longer pink, 4-5 minutes. Stir in butter until melted; sprinkle with flour. Gradually stir in the milk, salt and pepper. Bring to a boil, stirring constantly; cook and stir 2 minutes. Serve over biscuits.

1 BISCUIT WITH ⅓ CUP GRAVY: 454 cal., 27g fat (12g sat. fat), 72mg chol., 864mg sod., 36g carb. (7g sugars, 1g fiber), 16g pro.

DROP BISCUITS & GRAVY

A.M. RUSH ESPRESSO SMOOTHIE

Want an early-morning pick-me-up that's good for you, too? Fruit and flaxseed give this sweet espresso a nutritious twist.
—*Aimee Wilson, Clovis, CA*

- -

TAKES: 10 min. • **MAKES:** 1 serving

- ½ cup cold fat-free milk
- 1 Tbsp. vanilla flavoring syrup
- 1 cup ice cubes
- ½ medium banana, cut up
- 1 to 2 tsp. instant espresso powder
- 1 tsp. ground flaxseed
- 1 tsp. baking cocoa

In a blender, combine all ingredients; cover and process until blended, 1-2 minutes. Pour into a chilled glass; serve immediately.

NOTE: This recipe was tested with Torani brand flavoring syrup. Look for it in the coffee section of the grocery store.

1½ CUPS: 148 cal., 2g fat (0 sat. fat), 2mg chol., 54mg sod., 31g carb. (21g sugars, 3g fiber), 6g pro.

BERRY-TOPPED PUFF PANCAKE

Impressive to look at and even better to taste, this gorgeous pancake is surprisingly simple to make.
—*Marie Cosenza, Cortlandt Manor, NY*

PREP: 20 min. • **BAKE:** 15 min.
MAKES: 4 servings

- 2 Tbsp. butter
- 2 large eggs
- ½ cup 2% milk
- ½ cup all-purpose flour
- 2 Tbsp. sugar
- ¼ tsp. salt

TOPPING
- ⅓ cup sugar
- 1 Tbsp. cornstarch
- ½ cup orange juice
- 2 tsp. orange liqueur
- 1 cup sliced fresh strawberries
- 1 cup fresh blueberries
- 1 cup fresh raspberries
  Confectioners' sugar, optional

1. Place the butter in a 9-in. pie plate. Place in a 425° oven until melted, 4-5 minutes. Meanwhile, in a large bowl, whisk eggs and milk. In another bowl, combine the flour, sugar and salt. Whisk into egg mixture until blended. Pour into prepared pie plate. Bake until the sides are crisp and golden brown, 14-16 minutes.

2. Meanwhile, in a small saucepan, combine sugar and cornstarch. Gradually stir in the orange juice and liqueur. Bring to a boil over medium heat, stirring constantly. Cook and stir until thickened, 1-2 minutes longer. Remove from the heat.

3. Spoon berries over pancake, and drizzle with sauce. Dust with confectioners' sugar if desired.

1 SLICE: 320 cal., 9g fat (5g sat. fat), 123mg chol., 239mg sod., 54g carb. (35g sugars, 4g fiber), 7g pro.

MY TWO CENT$

"I love this recipe! It is so easy and yet looks like you really fussed, so it makes a perfect company breakfast. I didn't have orange liqueur so I used orange juice for both the juice and liqueur amounts. It worked great."
—DABAKER55126, TASTEOFHOME.COM

SAUSAGE BREAKFAST HASH

SAUSAGE BREAKFAST HASH

Served with dough well-done (toast) and dirty water (coffee), this fun, cheap and tasty diner classic is the perfect combo of breakfast staples.
—*Jacob Kitzman, Seattle, WA*

TAKES: 30 min. • **MAKES:** 4 servings

- 3 Tbsp. butter, divided
- 1 pkg. (20 oz.) refrigerated diced potatoes with onion
- 1 pkg. (7 oz.) frozen fully cooked breakfast sausage links, thawed and sliced
- 1 small green pepper, chopped
- 1 small sweet red pepper, chopped
- ¼ tsp. salt
  Dash cayenne pepper
- 1 cup shredded Swiss cheese
- 8 large eggs
- ¼ tsp. pepper
  Hot pepper sauce, optional

1. In a large skillet, melt 1 Tbsp. butter over medium heat; stir in the potatoes, sausage, green and red peppers, salt and cayenne. Cover and cook until the potatoes and the vegetables are tender, 12-14 minutes, stirring occasionally. Stir in cheese.

2. In a large skillet, fry eggs in the remaining butter as desired. Sprinkle with the pepper. Serve the eggs with the hash and, if desired, pepper sauce.

1 CUP POTATO MIXTURE WITH 2 EGGS: 621 cal., 45g fat (20g sat. fat), 501mg chol., 1251mg sod., 26g carb. (4g sugars, 2g fiber), 29g pro.

BERRY-TOPPED
PUFF PANCAKE

FAST FIX
HERB BREAKFAST FRITTATA

I came up with this recipe on a snowy day by using what I had in the fridge. A Yukon Gold potato gives it a comforting crust.
—*Katherine Hansen, Brunswick, ME*

TAKES: 30 min. • **MAKES:** 4 servings

- ¼ cup thinly sliced red onion
- 1 Tbsp. olive oil
- 1 large Yukon Gold potato, peeled and thinly sliced
- 6 large eggs
- 1 tsp. minced fresh rosemary or ¼ tsp. dried rosemary, crushed
- 1 tsp. minced fresh thyme or ¼ tsp. dried thyme
- ¼ tsp. salt
- ⅛ tsp. crushed red pepper flakes
- ⅛ tsp. pepper
- 2 Tbsp. shredded cheddar cheese

1. In an 8-in. ovenproof skillet, saute onion in oil until tender. Using a slotted spoon, remove onion and keep warm. Arrange potato slices in a single layer over bottom of pan. Preheat broiler.
2. In a small bowl, whisk the eggs, seasonings and onion; pour over potatoes. Cover and cook until nearly set, 4-6 minutes.
3. Uncover skillet. Broil 3-4 in. from the heat until eggs are completely set, 2-3 minutes. Sprinkle frittata with the cheese. Let stand for 5 minutes. Cut into wedges.

1 WEDGE: 204 cal., 12g fat (4g sat. fat), 321mg chol., 277mg sod., 13g carb. (2g sugars, 1g fiber), 11g pro. **DIABETIC EXCHANGES:** 1 starch, 1 medium-fat meat, 1 fat.

FAST FIX
SPICED PUMPKIN WARM-UP

Make this drink your own! You can add coffee if you want an extra kick. I've also chilled this mixture and blended it with vanilla ice cream to make it a pumpkin shake.
—*Andrea Heyart, Aubrey, TX*

TAKES: 10 min. • **MAKES:** 2 servings

- 2 cups half-and-half cream
- 3 Tbsp. sugar
- 2 Tbsp. canned pumpkin
- 1 tsp. pumpkin pie spice
- ¼ tsp. vanilla extract
  Whipped cream and additional pumpkin pie spice

In a small saucepan, combine cream, sugar, pumpkin and pie spice; cook and stir over medium heat until blended and heated through. Remove from heat; stir in vanilla. Top servings with whipped cream and additional pie spice.

1 CUP: 402 cal., 24g fat (16g sat. fat), 120mg chol., 121mg sod., 28g carb. (27g sugars, 1g fiber), 8g pro.

HERB BREAKFAST FRITTATA

BAKED FRENCH TOAST WITH BLUEBERRY SAUCE

DEBBIE JOHNSON
Centertown, MO

FAST FIX

LOW-FAT BREAKFAST BURRITOS

We're trying to eat healthier, so this recipe is the result of lightening up our favorite fast-food burritos. You can replace the sausage with ham or bacon.
—*Sandra Ward, Tulsa, OK*

- -

TAKES: 20 min. • **MAKES:** 4 servings

- 4 large eggs
- ¼ cup salsa
- ⅛ tsp. chili powder
- ⅛ tsp. ground cumin
- ⅛ tsp. pepper
- 3 breakfast turkey sausage links, casings removed
- ¼ cup shredded reduced-fat cheddar cheese
- 4 fat-free flour tortillas (6 in.), warmed

1. In a small bowl, whisk the eggs, salsa, chili powder, cumin and pepper; set aside.
2. Crumble the sausage into a large skillet; cook over medium heat until no longer pink. Drain. Push sausage to the sides of pan. Pour egg mixture into center of pan. Cook and stir until set. Sprinkle the cheddar cheese over the top. Remove from the heat; cover and let stand until cheese is melted.
3. Place ½ cup mixture on each tortilla; roll up. Serve warm.

1 BURRITO: 211 cal., 11g fat (4g sat. fat), 233mg chol., 510mg sod., 16g carb. (1g sugars, 1g fiber), 13g pro.

MY TWO CENT$

"What a tasty and versatile recipe. I sometimes make a 'grab-and-go' breakfast that we can take on the road with us. This one will be added to the rotation!"

—RENA 55, TASTEOFHOME.COM

BAKED FRENCH TOAST WITH BLUEBERRY SAUCE

French toast has a special-occasion feel, but why save it for company? Top it with a blueberry sauce to make any day festive.
—*Debbie Johnson, Centertown, MO*

- -

PREP: 20 min. • **BAKE:** 20 min.
MAKES: 4 servings (1 cup sauce)

- ¼ cup butter, melted
- 4 large eggs
- 1 cup 2% milk
- 1 tsp. vanilla extract
- ½ tsp. ground nutmeg
- 8 slices Texas toast

BLUEBERRY SAUCE
- ¼ cup sugar
- 1½ tsp. cornstarch
- ¼ tsp. ground cinnamon
- ⅛ tsp. ground cloves
- 1½ cups fresh or frozen blueberries
- 2 Tbsp. thawed orange juice concentrate

1. Pour melted butter into a 15x10x1-in. baking pan; lift and tilt pan to coat bottom evenly. In a large shallow bowl, whisk the eggs, milk, vanilla and nutmeg. Dip both sides of Texas toast into egg mixture; place on prepared pan. Bake toast at 375° until lightly browned, 20-25 minutes.
2. For sauce, in a large saucepan, combine the sugar, cornstarch, cinnamon and cloves. Stir in the blueberries and the orange juice concentrate. Bring to a boil; cook and stir until thickened, about 2 minutes. Serve with French toast.

2 SLICES FRENCH TOAST WITH ¼ CUP SAUCE: 481 cal., 20g fat (10g sat. fat), 225mg chol., 549mg sod., 63g carb. (27g sugars, 3g fiber), 14g pro.

ALMOND-BACON
CHEESE CROSTINI

APPETIZERS FOR LESS

It's true! You can host a great party without breaking your budget. Turn to this savory collection of nibbles the next time you're stocking an appetizer buffet, contributing a dish to pass or craving an easy snack. Let these 18 recipes show you how.

ALMOND-BACON CHEESE CROSTINI

Try these baked bites for a change from the usual toasted tomato appetizer. For a unique presentation, slice the baguette at an angle instead of making a straight cut.
—*Leondre Hermann, Stuart, FL*

PREP: 30 min. • **BAKE:** 15 min.
MAKES: 3 dozen

- 1 French bread baguette (1 lb.), cut into 36 slices
- 2 cups shredded Monterey Jack cheese
- ⅔ cup mayonnaise
- ½ cup sliced almonds, toasted
- 6 bacon strips, cooked and crumbled
- 1 green onion, chopped
  Dash salt
  Additional toasted almonds, optional

1. Place bread slices on an ungreased baking sheet. Bake at 400° until the bread is lightly browned, 8-9 minutes.
2. Meanwhile, in a large bowl, combine the cheese, mayonnaise, almonds, bacon, onion and salt. Spread over bread. Bake until the cheese is melted, 7-8 minutes. Sprinkle with additional almonds if desired. Serve warm.
1 CROSTINI: 120 cal., 8g fat (2g sat. fat), 8mg chol., 160mg sod., 10g carb. (0 sugars, 1g fiber), 3g pro.

SWEET GINGERED CHICKEN WINGS

FAST FIX
PARMESAN RANCH POPCORN

Make ho-hum popcorn worthy of a carnival with a savory seasoning blend.
—Taste of Home *Test Kitchen*

TAKES: 10 min. • **MAKES:** 3½ qt.

- ¼ cup grated Parmesan cheese
- 2 Tbsp. ranch salad dressing mix
- 1 tsp. dried parsley flakes
- ¼ tsp. onion powder
- ⅓ cup butter, melted
- 3½ qt. popped popcorn

Mix first four ingredients. Drizzle butter over popcorn; toss with cheese mixture. Store in airtight containers.
1 CUP: 112 cal., 10g fat (4g sat. fat), 13mg chol., 243mg sod., 6g carb. (0 sugars, 1g fiber), 1g pro.

SWEET GINGERED CHICKEN WINGS

When I make this recipe for a get-together, it's one of the first appetizers to disappear. I first tasted the delicious chicken wings years ago when I attended a class on using honey in cooking. Now I even use them as a main course.
—*Debbie Dougal, Roseville, CA*

PREP: 10 min. • **BAKE:** 1 hour
MAKES: 2 dozen

- 1 cup all-purpose flour
- 2 tsp. salt
- 2 tsp. paprika
- ¼ tsp. pepper
- 24 chicken wings (about 5 lbs.)
SAUCE
- ¼ cup honey
- ¼ cup thawed orange juice concentrate
- ½ tsp. ground ginger
  Minced fresh parsley, optional

1. Preheat oven to 350°. Line two baking sheets with foil; coat with cooking spray.
2. In a large shallow dish, combine flour, salt, paprika and pepper. Add chicken wings, a few at a time; turn to coat. Divide the wings between prepared pans. Bake 30 minutes.
3. In a small bowl, combine honey, orange juice concentrate and ginger; brush over chicken wings. Bake until juices run clear, 25-30 minutes.
4. Preheat broiler. Broil the wings 4 in. from the heat until lightly browned, 1-2 minutes. If desired, sprinkle with parsley.
1 CHICKEN WING: 134 cal., 7g fat (2g sat. fat), 29mg chol., 225mg sod., 8g carb. (4g sugars, 0 fiber), 10g pro.

BROCCOLI & CHIVE-STUFFED MINI PEPPERS

Crunchy peppers perfectly balance the creamy filling in these party appetizers. Fresh chives help them stand out.

—*Jean McKenzie, Vancouver, WA*

TAKES: 30 min. • **MAKES:** 2 dozen

12 miniature sweet peppers
1 pkg. (8 oz.) cream cheese, softened
⅓ cup minced fresh chives
⅛ tsp. salt
⅛ tsp. pepper
⅔ cup finely chopped fresh broccoli
⅔ cup shredded cheddar cheese

1. Preheat oven to 400°. Cut the peppers lengthwise in half; remove seeds. In a bowl, mix cream cheese, chives, salt and pepper; stir in broccoli. Spoon into pepper halves.
2. Place on a foil-lined baking sheet; bake until heated through, 9-11 minutes. Sprinkle with cheddar cheese. Bake until cheese is melted, 3-4 minutes longer. Cool slightly before serving.

1 STUFFED PEPPER HALF: 48 cal., 4g fat (2g sat. fat), 14mg chol., 68mg sod., 1g carb. (1g sugars, 0 fiber), 1g pro.

BUTTERY RADISH BAGUETTE

My dad and brother are crazy for radishes, and this peppery baguette appetizer is a big-time favorite. Add a sprinkle of fresh dill or parsley on top.

—*Kathy Hewitt, Cranston, RI*

TAKES: 15 min. • **MAKES:** about 1½ dozen

1 sourdough or French bread baguette (about 10 oz.), cut diagonally into ¾-in. slices
6 Tbsp. unsalted butter, softened
2¼ cups thinly sliced radishes (about 18 medium)
    Sea salt
    Snipped fresh dill, optional

Spread baguette slices with butter. Top with the radishes. Sprinkle lightly with salt and, if desired, top with dill.

1 BAGUETTE: 76 cal., 4g fat (2g sat. fat), 10mg chol., 107mg sod., 9g carb. (1g sugars, 0 fiber), 1g pro.

MINI PHYLLO TACOS

MINI PHYLLO TACOS

Crispy phyllo cups are the secret to creating an appetizer that has all the flavor and appeal of a taco but is much easier to eat. The two-bite treats of spicy ground beef and zesty shredded cheese will be a surefire hit with a hungry crowd.

—*Roseann Weston, Philipsburg, PA*

PREP: 30 min. • **BAKE:** 10 min.
MAKES: 2½ dozen

1 lb. lean ground beef (90% lean)
½ cup finely chopped onion
1 envelope taco seasoning
¾ cup water
1¼ cups shredded Mexican cheese blend, divided
2 pkg. (1.9 oz. each) frozen miniature phyllo tart shells

1. Preheat the oven to 350°. In a small skillet, cook beef and onion over medium heat until meat is no longer pink; drain. Stir in the taco seasoning and water. Bring to a boil. Reduce heat; simmer, uncovered, 5 minutes. Remove from heat; stir in ½ cup cheese blend.
2. Place the phyllo tart shells in an ungreased 15x10x1-in. baking pan. Fill with taco mixture.
3. Bake 6 minutes. Sprinkle with remaining cheese blend; bake until cheese is melted, 2-3 minutes longer.

FREEZE OPTION: Freeze cooled taco cups in a freezer container, separating layers with waxed paper. To use, reheat on a baking sheet in a preheated 350° oven until crisp and heated through.

1 SERVING: 63 cal., 3g fat (1g sat. fat), 11mg chol., 156mg sod., 4g carb. (0 sugars, 0 fiber), 4g pro.

BRAT & BACON APPETIZER PIZZA

Chopped bratwurst and maple bacon are a great way to start a pizza. I jazz it up even more with apricot preserves and honey mustard. The snack-size slices win over even the toughest critics.

—Colleen Vrooman, Waukesha, WI

TAKES: 25 min. • **MAKES:** 24 servings

- 1 tube (11 oz.) refrigerated thin pizza crust
- 4 maple-flavored bacon strips, chopped
- ¼ cup finely chopped onion
- 3 fully cooked beer bratwurst links, finely chopped
- ⅓ cup apricot preserves
- 2 tsp. honey mustard
- 2 cups shredded white or yellow cheddar cheese

1. Preheat oven to 400°. Unroll and press dough onto bottom and ½ in. up sides of a greased 15x10x1-in. baking pan. Bake until edges are lightly browned, 8-10 minutes.
2. Meanwhile, in a large skillet, cook bacon and onion over medium heat until bacon is crisp, stirring occasionally. Remove with a slotted spoon; drain on paper towels. Discard drippings. Add the bratwurst to same pan; cook and stir until browned, 2-3 minutes.
3. In a small bowl, mix the preserves and mustard. Spread over the crust; top with bratwurst, bacon mixture and cheese. Bake until cheese is melted, 8-10 minutes.
1 PIECE: 124 cal., 7g fat (3g sat. fat), 16mg chol., 229mg sod., 10g carb. (3g sugars, 0 fiber), 5g pro.

SAVORY POTATO SKINS

SAVORY POTATO SKINS

For a simple hot snack on your appetizer buffet, put together a plate of these crisp potato skins.

—Andrea Holcomb, Torrington, CT

PREP: 1¼ hours • **BROIL:** 5 min.
MAKES: 32 appetizers

- 4 large baking potatoes (about 12 oz. each)
- 3 Tbsp. butter, melted
- 1 tsp. salt
- 1 tsp. garlic powder
- 1 tsp. paprika
- Sour cream and chives, optional

1. Preheat oven to 375°. Scrub potatoes; pierce several times with a fork. Place on a greased baking sheet; bake until tender, 1-1¼ hours. Cool slightly.
2. Cut each potato lengthwise in half. Scoop out pulp, leaving ¼-in.-thick shells (save pulp for another use).
3. Cut each half potato shell lengthwise into quarters; return to baking sheet. Brush the insides with butter. Mix seasonings; sprinkle over butter.
4. Broil 4-5 in. from heat until golden brown, 5-8 minutes. If desired, mix sour cream and chives and serve with potato skins.
1 PIECE: 56 cal., 2g fat (1g sat. fat), 6mg chol., 168mg sod., 8g carb. (0 sugars, 1g fiber), 1g pro.

OUR TWO CENT$

Turn any leftover potato skins into an economical meal the next day. Just top the extra potato wedges with canned chili and shredded cheese. Then simply reheat it all in the microwave for a no-fuss lunch or dinner. Have some leftover taco meat? Toss that on top, too!

MINI MAC & CHEESE DOGS

We wanted to get creative with hot dogs, so we made a mac-and-cheesy version. Pile on the extra cheese, relish and even bacon.
—*Julie Peterson, Crofton, MD*

PREP: 25 min. + rising
BAKE: 20 min. + cooling • **MAKES:** 2 dozen

- 1 pkg. (16 oz.) frozen bread dough dinner rolls (12 count), thawed but still cold
- ½ cup panko (Japanese) bread crumbs
- 2 Tbsp. chopped onion
- 1 Tbsp. canola oil
- ¼ tsp. salt
- ⅛ tsp. pepper
- 12 bun-length beef hot dogs
- 1 pkg. (7¼ oz.) macaroni and cheese dinner mix

1. Let dough stand at room temperature until soft enough to shape, 15-20 minutes. Cut each roll in half; shape each half into a 3-in.-long mini hot dog bun. Place 2 in. apart on greased baking sheets.

2. Cover with greased plastic wrap; let rise in a warm place until almost doubled, about 45 minutes. Preheat oven to 350°.

3. Bake the buns until they are golden brown, 12-15 minutes. Remove from pans to wire racks to cool completely.

4. In a 15x10x1-in. baking pan, toss the bread crumbs with onion, oil, salt and pepper. Bake at 350° until golden brown, stirring once, 5-7 minutes.

5. Cook hot dogs and macaroni and cheese according to package directions. To serve, cut hot dogs crosswise in half. Split buns; fill with hot dogs and macaroni and cheese. Sprinkle with toasted crumbs.

1 APPETIZER: 198 cal., 12 g fat (5 g sat. fat), 25 mg chol., 446 mg sod., 18 g carb. (2 g sugars, 1 g fiber), 6 g pro.

DILL VEGETABLE DIP

A friend gave me this zesty dip recipe many years ago, and now I serve it at our annual holiday open house. To make it more readily portable, spoon a serving of the dip into the bottom of a disposable cup, then garnish with fresh veggies.
—*Karen Gardiner, Eutaw, AL*

PREP: 5 min. + chilling • **MAKES:** 1½ cups

- 1 cup sour cream
- ½ cup mayonnaise
- 1 Tbsp. finely chopped onion
- 2 tsp. dried parsley flakes
- 1 tsp. dill weed
- 1 tsp. seasoned salt
  Assorted fresh vegetables

Combine the first six ingredients; mix well. Cover and refrigerate. Serve with vegetables.
2 TBSP.: 107 cal., 11g fat (3g sat. fat), 17mg chol., 187mg sod., 1g carb. (1g sugars, 0 fiber), 1g pro.

MINI MAC & CHEESE DOGS

SWEET POTATO-CRUSTED CHICKEN NUGGETS

BLUE CHEESE POTATO CHIPS

Game day calls for something bold. I top potato chips with tomatoes, bacon and tangy blue cheese. I make two big pans, and they always disappear.
—*Bonnie Hawkins, Elkhorn, WI*

TAKES: 15 min. • **MAKES:** 10 servings

- 1 pkg. (8½ oz.) kettle-cooked potato chips
- 2 medium tomatoes, seeded and chopped
- 8 bacon strips, cooked and crumbled
- 6 green onions, chopped
- 1 cup crumbled blue cheese

1. Preheat broiler. In a 15x10x1-in. baking pan, arrange potato chips in an even layer. Top with remaining ingredients.
2. Broil 4-5 in. from heat until cheese begins to melt, 2-3 minutes. Serve immediately.
1 SERVING: 215 cal., 14g fat (5g sat. fat), 17mg chol., 359mg sod., 16g carb. (2g sugars, 1g fiber), 6g pro.

MEXICAN CHOCOLATE DIP

Chocolate, cinnamon and a touch of heat are a classic Mexican trio. Any fruit goes in this fudgy dip. And don't forget the churros!
—Taste of Home *Test Kitchen*

TAKES: 10 min. • **MAKES:** about ½ cup

- ¾ cup semisweet chocolate chips
- ⅓ cup heavy whipping cream
- ⅛ tsp. ground cinnamon
- ⅛ tsp. cayenne pepper
  Assorted fresh fruit

In a small heavy saucepan, combine the chocolate chips and cream. Using a whisk, heat and stir over medium-low heat until smooth, 4-5 minutes. Remove from heat; stir in cinnamon and cayenne. Cool slightly. Serve with fruit.
NOTE: Dip will become firmer as it cools. If desired, warm gently in the microwave to soften.
2 TBSP.: 221 cal., 17g fat (10g sat. fat), 27mg chol., 11mg sod., 21g carb. (18g sugars, 2g fiber), 2g pro.

FAST FIX
SWEET POTATO-CRUSTED CHICKEN NUGGETS

I was looking for ways to spice up traditional chicken nuggets and came up with this recipe. The chips add a crunchy texture and flavor while the meat is tender on the inside.
—*Kristina Segarra, Yonkers, NY*

TAKES: 30 min. • **MAKES:** 4 servings

  Oil for deep-fat frying
- 1 cup sweet potato chips
- ¼ cup all-purpose flour
- 1 tsp. salt, divided
- ½ tsp. coarsely ground pepper
- ¼ tsp. baking powder
- 1 Tbsp. cornstarch
- 1 lb. chicken tenderloins, cut into 1½-in. pieces

1. In an electric skillet or deep fryer, heat oil to 350°. Place chips, flour, ½ tsp. salt, pepper and baking powder in a food processor; pulse until ground. Transfer to a shallow dish.
2. Mix cornstarch and remaining salt; toss with chicken. Toss with potato chip mixture, pressing gently to coat.
3. Fry nuggets, a few at a time, until golden brown, 2-3 minutes. Drain on paper towels.
1 SERVING: 308 cal., 17g fat (1g sat. fat), 56mg chol., 690mg sod., 12g carb. (1g sugars, 1g fiber), 28g pro.

OUR TWO CENT$
If you're a dunker, try serving this with sweet-and-sour sauce. To reuse frying oil, cool oil and strain it to remove any food particles. Store, covered, in the refrigerator. Fry in small batches to maintain consistent oil temperature.

BLUE CHEESE
POTATO CHIPS

BONNIE HAWKINS
Elkorn, WI

ROASTED VEGETABLE DIP

While my children were always very good eaters, I came up with this recipe to get them to eat more veggies and like it. The dip doesn't last long in our house!
—*Sarah Vasques, Milford, NH*

- -

PREP: 15 min. • **BAKE:** 25 min. + cooling
MAKES: 20 servings

- 2 large sweet red peppers
- 1 large zucchini
- 1 medium onion
- 1 Tbsp. olive oil
- ½ tsp. salt
- ¼ tsp. pepper
- 1 pkg. (8 oz.) reduced-fat cream cheese
  Assorted crackers or fresh vegetables

1. Preheat oven to 425°. Cut vegetables into 1-in. pieces. Place in a 15x10x1-in. baking pan coated with cooking spray; toss with oil, salt and pepper. Roast until the vegetables are tender, stirring occasionally, 25-30 minutes. Cool completely.

2. Place vegetables and cream cheese in a food processor; process until blended. Transfer to a bowl; refrigerate, covered, until serving. Serve with assorted crackers or fresh vegetables.

HEALTH TIP: Roasted veggies account for more than half the volume of this blended dip, which means fewer calories, less saturated fat and more nutrients—not to mention amazing flavor.

2 TBSP. DIP: 44 cal., 3g fat (2g sat. fat), 8mg chol., 110mg sod., 3g carb. (2g sugars, 1g fiber), 2g pro.

FAST FIX | 5 INGREDIENTS

KICKIN' CAULIFLOWER

Try these savory bites for a spicy appetizer that's healthy, too!
—*Emily Tyra, Traverse City, MI*

- -

TAKES: 25 min. • **MAKES:** 8 servings

- 1 medium head cauliflower (about 2¼ lbs.), cut into florets
- 1 Tbsp. canola oil
- ½ cup Buffalo wing sauce
  Blue cheese salad dressing

1. Preheat oven to 400°. Toss the cauliflower with oil; spread in a 15x10x1-in. pan. Roast cauliflower until tender and lightly browned, 20-25 minutes, stirring once.

2. Transfer to a bowl; toss with wing sauce. Serve with dressing.

⅓ CUP: 39 cal., 2g fat (0 sat. fat), 0 chol., 474mg sod., 5g carb. (2g sugars, 2g fiber), 2g pro.

ROASTED VEGETABLE DIP

SARAH VASQUES
Milford, NH

SPICY EDAMAME

BUFFALO CHICKEN POCKETS

Here's my idea of pub food made easy: biscuits flavored with Buffalo wing sauce and blue cheese. They're my favorite for weekend parties.
—*Maria Regakis, Saugus, MA*

TAKES: 30 min. • **MAKES:** 8 servings

- ¾ **lb. ground chicken**
- ⅓ **cup Buffalo wing sauce**
- 1 **tube (16.3 oz.) large refrigerated buttermilk biscuits**
- ½ **cup shredded cheddar cheese**
  Blue cheese salad dressing, optional

1. Preheat oven to 375°. In a large skillet, cook chicken over medium heat until no longer pink, 5-7 minutes, breaking into crumbles; drain. Remove from heat; stir in wing sauce.
2. On a lightly floured surface, roll each biscuit into a 6-in. circle; top each with ¼ cup chicken mixture and 2 Tbsp. cheese. Fold dough over filling; pinch edge to seal.
3. Transfer to an ungreased baking sheet. Bake until golden brown, 12-14 minutes. If desired, serve with blue cheese dressing.
FREEZE OPTION: Freeze cooled pockets in a freezer container. To use, reheat pockets on an ungreased baking sheet in a preheated 375° oven until heated through.
1 POCKET: 258 cal., 12g fat (5g sat. fat), 35mg chol., 987mg sod., 25g carb. (3g sugars, 1g fiber), 12g pro.

SPICY EDAMAME

Edamame (pronounced ay-duh-MAH-may) are young soybeans in their pods. In our Test Kitchen, we boiled and seasoned them to create a unique finger food.
—*Taste of Home Test Kitchen*

TAKES: 20 min. • **MAKES:** 6 servings

- 1 **pkg. (16 oz.) frozen edamame pods**
- 2 **tsp. kosher salt**
- ¾ **tsp. ground ginger**
- ½ **tsp. garlic powder**
- ¼ **tsp. crushed red pepper flakes**

Place edamame in a large saucepan and cover with water. Bring to a boil. Cover and cook until edamame are tender, 4-5 minutes; drain. Transfer to a large bowl. Add the four seasonings; toss to coat.
1 SERVING: 52 cal., 2g fat (0 sat. fat), 0 chol., 642mg sod., 5g carb. (1g sugars, 2g fiber), 4g pro.

BLT BITES

These quick hors d'oeuvres may be mini, but their bacon and tomato flavor is full size. I serve them at parties, brunches and picnics, and they're always very popular. Even my kids love them.
—*Kellie Remmen, Detroit Lakes, MN*

PREP: 25 min. + chilling
MAKES: 16-20 appetizers

- 16 **to 20 cherry tomatoes**
- 1 **lb. sliced bacon, cooked and crumbled**
- ½ **cup mayonnaise**
- ⅓ **cup chopped green onions**
- 3 **Tbsp. grated Parmesan cheese**
- 2 **Tbsp. snipped fresh parsley**

1. Cut a thin slice off each tomato top. Scoop out and discard pulp. Invert the tomatoes on a paper towel to drain.
2. In a small bowl, combine the remaining ingredients. Spoon into the tomatoes. Refrigerate for several hours.
1 STUFFED TOMATO: 113 cal., 10g fat (3g sat. fat), 11mg chol., 206mg sod., 1g carb. (1g sugars, 0 fiber), 3g pro.

CAJUN CHICKEN & PASTA

AFFORDABLE ENTREES: BEEF, CHICKEN & TURKEY

Dig in! Just because you're saving money doesn't mean you can't savor hearty entrees. These 26 main courses pack on flavor without taxing your wallet, so enjoy a stick-to-your-ribs beef or poultry dinner tonight.

CAJUN CHICKEN & PASTA

This kicked-up pasta dish is a family favorite and my most requested recipe. It's easy to adapt, too. Swap in shrimp for the chicken, add your favorite veggies and adjust the spice level to your family's taste. You simply can't go wrong!

—Dolly Kragel, Smithland, IA

- -

PREP: 10 min. + standing • **COOK:** 35 min.
MAKES: 6 servings

- 1 lb. boneless skinless chicken breasts, cut into 2x½-in. strips
- 3 tsp. Cajun seasoning
- 8 oz. uncooked penne pasta (about 2⅓ cups)
- 2 Tbsp. butter, divided
- 1 small sweet red pepper, diced
- 1 small green pepper, diced
- ½ cup sliced fresh mushrooms
- 4 green onions, chopped
- 1 cup heavy whipping cream
- ½ tsp. salt
- ¼ tsp. dried basil
- ¼ tsp. lemon-pepper seasoning
- ¼ tsp. garlic powder
  Pepper to taste
  Chopped plum tomatoes
  Minced fresh basil
  Shredded Parmesan cheese

1. Toss chicken with Cajun seasoning; let stand 15 minutes. Cook pasta according to package directions; drain.
2. In a skillet, heat 1 Tbsp. butter over medium-high heat; saute chicken until no longer pink, 5-6 minutes. Remove from pan.
3. In same pan, heat remaining butter over medium-high; saute peppers, mushrooms and green onions until the peppers are crisp-tender, 6-8 minutes. Stir in cream and seasonings; bring to a boil. Cook and stir until slightly thickened, 4-6 minutes. Stir in pasta and chicken; heat through. Top with tomatoes and basil. Sprinkle with cheese.
1 SERVING: 398 cal., 21g fat (12g sat. fat), 97mg chol., 357mg sodium, 31g carb. (4g sugars, 2g fiber), 22g pro.

POTLUCK
TACO SALAD

FAST FIX
POTLUCK TACO SALAD

I found this recipe in an old cookbook, and I've taken the entree salad to many potlucks since then. I think the layers look so pretty in a glass bowl.

—Sandy Fynaardt, New Sharon, IA

- -

TAKES: 25 min.
MAKES: 8 servings (1 cup dressing)

- 1 lb. ground beef
- 1 envelope taco seasoning, divided
- 1 medium head iceberg lettuce, torn
- 1 can (16 oz.) kidney beans, rinsed and drained
- 1 large red onion, chopped
- 4 medium tomatoes, seeded and finely chopped
- 2 cups shredded cheddar cheese
- 4 cups crushed tortilla chips (about 8 oz.)
- 1 bottle (8 oz.) Thousand Island salad dressing
- 2 Tbsp. taco sauce

1. In a large skillet, cook and crumble the beef over medium heat until beef is no longer pink, 6-8 minutes; drain. Stir in 3 Tbsp. taco seasoning.
2. In a large bowl, layer beef mixture, lettuce, beans, onion, tomatoes, cheese and crushed chips. In a small bowl, mix the salad dressing, taco sauce and remaining taco seasoning; serve with salad.
1½ CUPS SALAD WITH 2 TBSP.
DRESSING: 574 cal., 34g fat (11g sat. fat), 66mg chol., 1109mg sod., 44g carb. (9g sugars, 5g fiber), 23g pro.

MY TWO CENT$

"I've made this for years now—for my family, lunches for colleagues and parties. Everyone raves about it and wants the recipe. It's the sauce that makes it different from any other taco salad. It's a surefire hit."
—MAGICKAT_CT, TASTEOFHOME.COM

**FAVORITE BAKED
SPAGHETTI**

FAVORITE BAKED SPAGHETTI

This tasty spaghetti casserole is always requested for our family gatherings. It's especially popular with my grandchildren, who just love all the cheese.
—*Louise Miller, Westminster, MD*

- -

PREP: 25 min. • **BAKE:** 1 hour
MAKES: 10 servings

- 1 pkg. (16 oz.) spaghetti
- 1 lb. ground beef
- 1 medium onion, chopped
- 1 jar (24 oz.) meatless spaghetti sauce
- ½ tsp. seasoned salt
- 2 large eggs
- ⅓ cup grated Parmesan cheese
- 5 Tbsp. butter, melted
- 2 cups 4% cottage cheese
- 4 cups part-skim shredded mozzarella cheese

1. Cook spaghetti according to the package directions. Meanwhile, in a large skillet, cook beef and onion over medium heat until meat is no longer pink; drain. Stir in the spaghetti sauce and seasoned salt; set aside.
2. In a large bowl, whisk the eggs, Parmesan cheese and butter. Drain spaghetti; add to egg mixture and toss to coat.
3. Place half of the spaghetti mixture in a greased 13x9-in. or 3-qt. baking dish. Top with half of the cottage cheese, meat sauce and mozzarella cheese. Repeat layers.
4. Cover and bake at 350° for 40 minutes. Uncover; bake until the cheese is melted, 20-25 minutes longer.
1¼ CUPS: 526 cal., 24g fat (13g sat. fat), 127mg chol., 881mg sod., 45g carb. (9g sugars, 3g fiber), 31g pro.

OUR TWO CENT$
Our Test Kitchen recommends using small-curd cottage cheese because it will meld right into baked dishes such as this, offering a smooth, creamy texture. For an even saucier experience, add a bit of extra sauce, or keep the casserole covered throughout baking.

SLOPPY JOES

FAST FIX
SLOPPY JOES

Everybody at the table will clamor over the zesty flavor of this yummy comfort food. Try it spooned over warmed cornbread if you don't have sandwich buns.
—*Karen Anderson, Cuyahoga Falls, OH*

- -

TAKES: 30 min. • **MAKES:** 6 servings

- 1½ lbs. ground beef
- 1 can (10 oz.) diced tomatoes and green chilies, undrained
- 1 can (6 oz.) tomato paste
- ¼ cup ketchup
- 2 Tbsp. brown sugar
- 1 Tbsp. spicy brown mustard
- ¼ tsp. salt
- 6 sandwich buns, split
  Fresh arugula, optional

In a large skillet, cook beef over medium heat until no longer pink; drain. Stir in the tomatoes, tomato paste, ketchup, brown sugar, mustard and salt. Bring to a boil. Reduce the heat; simmer, uncovered, for 5 minutes. Serve on buns. If desired, top with arugula.
FREEZE OPTION: Freeze the cooled meat mixture in freezer containers. To use, partially thaw in refrigerator overnight. Heat through in a saucepan, stirring occasionally and adding a little water if necessary. Serve on buns. If desired, top with arugula.
1 SANDWICH: 478 cal., 18g fat (6g sat. fat), 70mg chol., 918mg sod., 49g carb. (15g sugars, 2g fiber), 30g pro.

THAI PEANUT CHICKEN & NOODLES

This quick chicken recipe is very similar to chicken pad thai but is easier to make and cheaper than dining out. Rice noodles can be replaced with mung bean noodles or any type of egg noodles.

—*Kristina Segarra, Yonkers, NY*

TAKES: 30 min. • **MAKES:** 4 servings

½	cup water
¼	cup soy sauce
2	Tbsp. rice vinegar
2	Tbsp. creamy peanut butter
3	garlic cloves, minced
1	to 2 tsp. Sriracha Asian hot chili sauce
1	tsp. sesame oil
1	tsp. molasses
1	pkg. (6.75 oz.) thin rice noodles
2	Tbsp. peanut oil, divided
1	lb. chicken tenderloins, cut into ¾-in. pieces
1	medium onion, chopped
	Halved cucumber slices and chopped peanuts, optional

1. For sauce, whisk together the first eight ingredients. Bring a large saucepan of water to a boil; remove from heat. Add noodles; let stand until noodles are tender but firm, 3-4 minutes. Drain; rinse with cold water and drain well.

2. In a large skillet, heat 1 Tbsp. peanut oil over medium-high heat; saute the chicken until no longer pink, 5-7 minutes. Remove from pan.

3. In same pan, saute onion in remaining oil over medium-high heat until tender, 2-3 minutes. Stir in sauce; cook and stir over medium heat until slightly thickened. Add noodles and chicken; heat through, tossing to combine. If desired, top with cucumber and chopped peanuts. Serve immediately.

2 CUPS: 444 cal., 13g fat (2g sat. fat), 56mg chol., 1270mg sod., 48g carb. (6g sugars, 2g fiber), 34g pro.

SWEET CHILI & ORANGE CHICKEN

SWEET CHILI & ORANGE CHICKEN

My husband loves this chicken dish so much he often requests it when he comes home from deployment. The sweet chili sauce adds just the right amount of heat to the bright, citrusy sauce.

—*Jessica Eastman, Bremerton, WA*

TAKES: 20 min. • **MAKES:** 4 servings

1	lb. boneless skinless chicken breasts, cut into 1-in. pieces
¼	tsp. salt
¼	tsp. pepper
2	Tbsp. butter
¾	cup sweet chili sauce
⅓	cup thawed orange juice concentrate
	Hot cooked jasmine or other rice
	Minced fresh basil

1. Toss chicken with salt and pepper. In a large skillet, heat butter over medium-high heat; stir-fry chicken until no longer pink, 5-7 minutes. Remove from pan; keep warm.

2. Add chili sauce and juice concentrate to skillet; cook and stir until heated through. Stir in the chicken. Serve with rice; sprinkle with basil.

½ CUP CHICKEN MIXTURE: 309 cal., 9g fat (4g sat. fat), 78mg chol., 1014mg sod., 33g carb. (31g sugars, 1g fiber), 24g pro.

SOUTHWESTERN CASSEROLE

I've been making this family-pleasing casserole for years. It tastes wonderful, fits nicely into our budget and, best of all, makes a second to freeze and enjoy later.
—*Joan Hallford, North Richland Hills, TX*

PREP: 25 min. • **BAKE:** 40 min.
MAKES: 2 casseroles (6 servings each)

- 2 cups (8 oz.) uncooked elbow macaroni
- 2 lbs. ground beef
- 1 large onion, chopped
- 2 garlic cloves, minced
- 2 cans (14½ oz. each) diced tomatoes, undrained
- 1 can (16 oz.) kidney beans, rinsed and drained
- 1 can (6 oz.) tomato paste
- 1 can (4 oz.) chopped green chilies, drained
- 1½ tsp. salt
- 1 tsp. chili powder
- ½ tsp. ground cumin
- ½ tsp. pepper
- 2 cups shredded Monterey Jack cheese
- 2 jalapeno peppers, seeded and chopped

1. Cook macaroni according to package directions. Meanwhile, in a large saucepan, cook beef and onion over medium heat, crumbling beef, until meat is no longer pink. Add garlic; cook 1 minute longer. Drain. Stir in the next eight ingredients. Bring to a boil. Reduce the heat; simmer, uncovered, for 10 minutes. Drain the macaroni; stir into the beef mixture.

2. Preheat oven to 375°. Transfer macaroni mixture to two greased 2-qt. baking dishes. Top with cheese and jalapenos. Cover and bake at 375° for 30 minutes. Uncover; bake until bubbly and heated through, about 10 minutes longer. Serve one casserole. Cool the second casserole; cover and freeze up to 3 months.

TO USE FROZEN CASSEROLE: Thaw in refrigerator 8 hours. Preheat oven to 375°. Remove from refrigerator 30 minutes before baking. Cover casserole and bake, increasing the time as necessary to heat through and for a thermometer inserted in center to read 165°, 20-25 minutes.

NOTE: Wear disposable gloves when cutting hot peppers; the oils can burn skin. Avoid touching your face.

1 CUP: 321 cal., 15g fat (7g sat. fat), 64mg chol., 673mg sod., 23g carb. (5g sugars, 4g fiber), 24g pro.

SOUTHWESTERN CASSEROLE

JOAN HALLFORD
North Richlands Hills, TX

FAST FIX | 5 INGREDIENTS

GNOCCHI CHICKEN SKILLET

Potato gnocchi are little dumplings made from a dough of potatoes, flour and sometimes eggs. Look for gnocchi in the pasta, ethnic or frozen section of your grocery store.
—*Taste of Home Test Kitchen*

TAKES: 20 min. • **MAKES:** 4 servings

- 1 pkg. (16 oz.) potato gnocchi
- 1 lb. ground chicken
- ½ cup chopped onion
- 2 Tbsp. olive oil
- 1 jar (26 oz.) spaghetti sauce
- ¼ tsp. salt
- ¼ to ½ tsp. dried oregano
  Shredded Parmesan cheese, optional

1. Cook gnocchi according to the package directions. Meanwhile, in a large skillet, cook chicken and onion in oil over medium heat until the chicken is no longer pink; drain if necessary. Stir in the spaghetti sauce, salt and oregano; cook until heated through, 5-10 minutes.

2. Drain gnocchi; gently stir into skillet. Garnish servings with cheese if desired.

1½ CUPS: 598 cal., 24g fat (6g sat. fat), 88mg chol., 1632mg sod., 66g carb. (19g sugars, 6g fiber), 30g pro.

STUFFED PEPPERS
FOR FOUR

ONE-PAN CHICKEN RICE CURRY

I've been loving the subtle spice from curry lately, so I incorporated it into this saucy chicken and rice dish. It's a one-pan meal that's become a go-to dinnertime favorite.
—*Mary Lou Timpson, Colorado City, AZ*

- -

TAKES: 30 min. • **MAKES:** 4 servings

- 2 **Tbsp. butter, divided**
- 1 **medium onion, halved and thinly sliced**
- 2 **Tbsp. all-purpose flour**
- 3 **tsp. curry powder**
- ½ **tsp. salt**
- ½ **tsp. pepper**
- 1 **lb. boneless skinless chicken breasts, cut into 1-in. pieces**
- 1 **can (14½ oz.) reduced-sodium chicken broth**
- 1 **cup uncooked instant rice** **Chopped fresh cilantro leaves, optional**

1. In a large nonstick skillet, heat 1 Tbsp. butter over medium-high heat; saute the onion until tender and lightly browned, 3-5 minutes. Remove from pan.
2. In a bowl, mix flour and seasonings; toss with chicken. In same skillet, heat remaining butter over medium-high heat. Add chicken; cook just until no longer pink, 4-6 minutes, turning occasionally.
3. Stir in the broth and onion; bring to a boil. Stir in the rice. Remove from heat; let stand, covered, 5 minutes (mixture will be saucy). If desired, sprinkle with cilantro.
1 CUP: 300 cal., 9g fat (4g sat. fat), 78mg chol., 658mg sod., 27g carb. (2g sugars, 2g fiber), 27g pro. **DIABETIC EXCHANGES:** 3 lean meat, 2 starch, 1½ fat.

STUFFED PEPPERS FOR FOUR

Truly a meal-in-one recipe, this quick supper has it all: veggies, meat, pasta and sauce, packed into tender peppers. It cuts costs and looks so pretty on the table.
—*Taste of Home Test Kitchen*

- -

TAKES: 30 min. • **MAKES:** 4 servings

- ½ **cup uncooked orzo pasta**
- 4 **medium sweet peppers (any color)**
- ¼ **cup water**
- 1 **lb. ground beef**
- ½ **cup chopped onion**
- 2 **cups pasta sauce**
- 1 **cup frozen broccoli-cauliflower blend, thawed and chopped**
- ½ **cup grated Parmesan cheese, divided**

1. Cook the orzo according to the package directions; drain. Cut and discard tops from peppers; remove seeds. Place in a 3-qt. ~~~rowave-safe dish. Add water; ~~~ered, on high until peppers ~~~er, 7-9 minutes.

2. In a skillet, cook and crumble the beef with onion over medium heat until no longer pink, 5-7 minutes; drain. Stir in the pasta sauce, vegetables, ¼ cup cheese and orzo. Spoon into peppers. Sprinkle with the remaining Parmesan cheese.
3. Microwave, uncovered, on high until heated through, 1-2 minutes.
1 STUFFED PEPPER: 448 cal., 18g fat (7g sat. fat), 79mg chol., 734mg sod., 41g carb. (15g sugars, 6g fiber), 30g pro.

MY TWO CENT$

"This stuffed pepper recipe is really delicious. I never made it with pasta sauce before, and it's different but very good."

—NLFPA, TASTEOFHOME.COM

ONE-PAN CHICKEN
RICE CURRY

GARLIC-GINGER TURKEY TENDERLOINS

This good-for-you entree can be on your family's dinner plates quicker than Chinese takeout—and for a lot less money! Ginger and brown sugar flavor the sauce that spices up the turkey as it bakes.
—Taste of Home *Test Kitchen*

TAKES: 30 min. • **MAKES:** 4 servings

- 3 Tbsp. brown sugar, divided
- 2 Tbsp. plus 2 tsp. reduced-sodium soy sauce, divided
- 2 Tbsp. minced fresh gingerroot
- 6 garlic cloves, minced
- ½ tsp. pepper
- 1 pkg. (20 oz.) turkey breast tenderloins
- 1 Tbsp. cornstarch
- 1 cup reduced-sodium chicken broth

1. Preheat oven to 375°. In a small saucepan, mix 2 Tbsp. brown sugar, 2 Tbsp. soy sauce, ginger, garlic and pepper.
2. Place the turkey in a 13x9-in. baking dish coated with cooking spray; drizzle with half of the soy sauce mixture. Bake the turkey, uncovered, until a thermometer reads 165°, 25-30 minutes.
3. Meanwhile, add the cornstarch and the remaining brown sugar and soy sauce to the remaining mixture in saucepan; stir until smooth. Stir in broth. Bring to a boil; cook and stir until thickened, 1-2 minutes. Cut turkey into slices; serve with sauce.
4 OZ. COOKED TURKEY WITH 2 TBSP. SAUCE: 212 cal., 2g fat (1g sat. fat), 69mg chol., 639mg sod., 14g carb. (10g sugars, 0 fiber), 35g pro. **DIABETIC EXCHANGES:** 4 lean meat, 1 starch.

CREAMY DIJON CHICKEN

You'll save both time and money with this chicken dish. It makes a nice sauce that works well over brown rice or wide noodles. If you want extra sauce for leftovers, simply double the recipe.
—Irene Boffo, Fountain Hills, AZ

TAKES: 25 min. • **MAKES:** 4 servings

- ½ cup half-and-half cream
- ¼ cup Dijon mustard
- 1 Tbsp. brown sugar
- 4 boneless skinless chicken breast halves (6 oz. each)
- ¼ tsp. salt
- ¼ tsp. pepper
- 2 tsp. olive oil
- 2 tsp. butter
- 1 small onion, halved and very thinly sliced
  Minced fresh parsley

1. Whisk together the cream, mustard and brown sugar. Pound chicken breasts with a meat mallet to even thickness; sprinkle with salt and pepper.
2. In a large skillet, heat oil and butter over medium-high heat; brown chicken on both sides. Reduce heat to medium. Add onion and the cream mixture; bring to a boil. Reduce the heat; simmer, covered, until a thermometer inserted in the chicken reads 165°, 10-12 minutes. Sprinkle with parsley.
1 CHICKEN BREAST HALF WITH 3 TBSP. SAUCE: 295 cal., 11g fat (5g sat. fat), 114mg chol., 621mg sod., 6g carb. (5g sugars, 0 fiber), 36g pro. **DIABETIC EXCHANGES:** 5 lean meat, 1 fat, ½ starch.

CREAMY DIJON CHICKEN

CHICKEN TACO PIE

A true family favorite, this dish is just perfect for a busy night of rushing off to soccer, swimming lessons or Scouts. I put it together in the morning, refrigerate it and pop it in the oven when I get home.
—*Karen Latimer, Winnipeg, MB*

- -

PREP: 20 min. • **BAKE:** 30 min.
MAKES: 6 servings

- 1 tube (8 oz.) refrigerated crescent rolls
- 1 lb. ground chicken
- 1 envelope taco seasoning
- 1 can (4 oz.) chopped green chilies
- ½ cup water
- ½ cup salsa
- ½ cup shredded Mexican cheese blend
- 1 cup shredded lettuce
- 1 small sweet red pepper, chopped
- 1 small green pepper, chopped
- 1 medium tomato, seeded and chopped
- 1 green onion, thinly sliced
- 2 Tbsp. pickled jalapeno slices
  Sour cream and additional salsa

1. Preheat oven to 350°. Unroll crescent dough and separate into triangles. Press onto bottom of a greased 9-in. pie plate to form a crust, sealing seams well. Bake until golden brown, 18-20 minutes.
2. Meanwhile, in a large skillet, cook chicken over medium heat until chicken is no longer pink, breaking into crumbles, 6-8 minutes; drain. Stir in taco seasoning, green chilies, water and salsa; bring to a boil.
3. Spoon into crust; sprinkle with cheese. Bake until cheese is melted, 8-10 minutes.
4. Top with lettuce, peppers, tomato, green onion and pickled jalapeno. Serve with sour cream and additional salsa.
1 SLICE: 328 cal., 17 g fat (6 g sat. fat), 58 mg chol., 1122 mg sod., 25 g carb. (5 g sugars, 1 g fiber), 17 g pro.

OUR TWO CENT$
Save money when you swap out the ground chicken with last night's leftover shredded or cubed chicken or turkey. Ground beef works equally well.

ZUCCHINI BEEF SKILLET

FAST FIX
ZUCCHINI BEEF SKILLET
This speedy recipe helps use up everyone's favorite garden goodies: zucchini, tomatoes and green peppers.
—*Becky Calder, Kingston, MO*

- -

TAKES: 30 min. • **MAKES:** 4 servings

- 1 lb. ground beef
- 1 medium onion, chopped
- 1 small green pepper, chopped
- 2 tsp. chili powder
- ¾ tsp. salt
- ¼ tsp. pepper
- 3 medium zucchini, cut into ¾-in. cubes
- 2 large tomatoes, chopped
- ¼ cup water
- 1 cup uncooked instant rice
- 1 cup shredded cheddar cheese

1. In a large skillet, cook and crumble beef with onion and pepper over medium-high heat until no longer pink, 5-7 minutes; drain.
2. Stir in seasonings, vegetables, water and rice; bring to a boil. Reduce heat; simmer, covered, until rice is tender, 10-15 minutes. Sprinkle with cheese. Remove from heat; let stand until cheese is melted.
2 CUPS: 470 cal., 24g fat (11g sat. fat), 98mg chol., 749mg sod., 33g carb. (8g sugars, 4g fiber), 32g pro.

EFFORTLESS
ALFREDO PIZZA

EFFORTLESS ALFREDO PIZZA

Here's a lighter, scrumptious twist for family pizza night. The recipe makes good use of leftovers and convenience items, so I don't have to spend much time in the kitchen. I often use collard greens instead of spinach.
—*Brittney House, Lockport, IL*

- -

TAKES: 20 min. • **MAKES:** 6 slices

- 1   pkg. (10 oz.) frozen chopped spinach, thawed and squeezed dry
- 1   cup shredded cooked turkey breast
- 2   tsp. lemon juice
- ¼   tsp. salt
- ¼   tsp. pepper
- 1   prebaked 12-in. pizza crust
- 1   garlic clove, peeled and halved
- ½   cup reduced-fat Alfredo sauce
- ¾   cup shredded fontina cheese
- ½   tsp. crushed red pepper flakes

1. Preheat oven to 450°. In a large bowl, mix the first five ingredients until blended.
2. Place crust on an ungreased 12-in. pizza pan; rub with cut sides of garlic. Discard garlic. Spread Alfredo sauce over crust. Top with spinach mixture, cheese and pepper flakes. Bake until crust is lightly browned, 8-12 minutes.
1 SLICE: 302 cal., 10g fat (4g sat. fat), 45mg chol., 756mg sod., 33g carb. (1g sugars, 1g fiber), 20g pro. **DIABETIC EXCHANGES:** 2 starch, 2 lean meat, ½ fat.

MY TWO CENT$

"Made this for my book club's potluck, and it was a smash hit. I topped half with turkey and half with chicken. It was very quick and several people asked for the recipe afterward!"
—NLFPA, TASTEOFHOME.COM

BUFFALO CHICKEN TENDERS

BUFFALO CHICKEN TENDERS

These chicken tenders get a spicy kick thanks to a homemade Buffalo sauce. They taste as if they're from a restaurant, but are so easy to make at home. Blue cheese dipping sauce takes them over the top.
—*Dahlia Abrams, Detroit, MI*

- -

TAKES: 20 min. • **MAKES:** 4 servings

- 1   lb. chicken tenderloins
- 2   Tbsp. all-purpose flour
- ¼   tsp. pepper
- 2   Tbsp. butter, divided
- ⅓   cup Louisiana-style hot sauce
- 1¼   tsp. Worcestershire sauce
- 1   tsp. minced fresh oregano
- ½   tsp. garlic powder
      Blue cheese salad dressing, optional

1. Toss the chicken with flour and pepper. In a large skillet, heat 1 Tbsp. butter over medium heat. Add chicken; cook until no longer pink, 4-6 minutes per side. Remove from pan.
2. In a small bowl, mix the hot sauce, Worcestershire sauce, oregano and garlic powder. In same skillet, melt the remaining butter; stir in sauce mixture. Add chicken; heat through, turning to coat. If desired, serve with blue cheese dressing.
1 SERVING: 184 cal., 7g fat (4g sat. fat), 71mg chol., 801mg sod., 5g carb. (1g sugars, 0 fiber), 27g pro. **DIABETIC EXCHANGES:** 3 lean meat, 1½ fat.

MEXI-MAC CASSEROLE

I typically have most of the ingredients for this dish in my pantry. Green chilies give it a little bite, but it's easy to swap in a can of spicier tomatoes to turn up the heat.
—Janice Conklin, Stevensville, MT

- -

PREP: 25 min. • **BAKE:** 30 min.
MAKES: 8 servings

- 1 pkg. (7¼ oz.) macaroni
     and cheese dinner mix
- 1½ lbs. lean ground beef (90% lean)
- 1 medium onion, finely chopped
- 2 garlic cloves, minced
- 1 can (14½ oz.) diced tomatoes
     with mild green chilies
- 1 can (4 oz.) chopped green chilies
- 1 envelope reduced-sodium
     taco seasoning
- 2½ cups shredded Mexican
     cheese blend, divided
- 1 can (16 oz.) kidney beans,
     rinsed and drained
- 1 can (15¼ oz.) whole
     kernel corn, drained
- 1 can (7¾ oz.) Mexican-style
     hot tomato sauce
- ½ cup crushed tortilla chips

1. Prepare the macaroni and cheese mix according to package directions. Meanwhile, cook the beef, onion and garlic in a Dutch oven over medium heat until meat is no longer pink; drain.

2. Add the diced tomatoes, green chilies and taco seasoning. Stir in 2 cups cheese, beans, corn, tomato sauce and prepared macaroni and cheese dinner.

3. Transfer to a greased 13x9-in. baking dish; sprinkle with chips and remaining cheese.

4. Bake, uncovered, at 350° until bubbly, 30-35 minutes.

FREEZE OPTION: Cool unbaked casserole; cover and freeze. To use, partially thaw in the refrigerator overnight. Remove from the refrigerator 30 minutes before baking. Preheat oven to 350°. Bake casserole as directed, increasing time as necessary to heat through and for a thermometer inserted in center to read 165°.

1½ CUPS: 555 cal., 27g fat (13g sat. fat), 106mg chol., 1333mg sod., 45g carb. (11g sugars, 6g fiber), 33g pro.

CHEESY BOW TIE CHICKEN

SALLY SIBTHORPE
Shelby Township, MI

FAST FIX | 5 INGREDIENTS

CHEESY BOW TIE CHICKEN

Here's a super simple dish that tastes as if it's straight from a nice Italian restaurant. Spinach-artichoke dip is usually available in a store's frozen foods section, but you might also find it in a supermarket deli.
—Sally Sibthorpe, Shelby Township, MI

- -

TAKES: 30 min. • **MAKES:** 4 servings

- 2 pkg. (8 oz. each) frozen spinach
     and artichoke cheese dip
- 3 cups uncooked bow tie pasta
- 3 cups cubed rotisserie chicken
- 1 cup chopped roasted
     sweet red peppers
- ⅓ cup pitted Greek olives, halved
- ½ tsp. salt
- ¼ tsp. pepper

1. Heat cheese dip according to the package directions. Meanwhile, in a Dutch oven, cook pasta according to package directions; drain, reserving ½ cup pasta water. Return to pan.

2. Stir in chicken, cheese dip, peppers, olives, salt and pepper, adding enough reserved pasta water to reach a creamy consistency; heat through.

1½ CUPS: 453 cal., 12g fat (3g sat. fat), 93mg chol., 795mg sod., 44g carb. (4g sugars, 2g fiber), 38g pro.

CASSOULET FOR TODAY

Rustic French cassoulet is traditionally cooked for hours, but this version offers the same homey taste in less time. It's easy on the wallet, too.

—*Virginia Anthony, Jacksonville, FL*

PREP: 45 min. • **BAKE:** 50 min.
MAKES: 6 servings

6   boneless skinless chicken
    thighs (about 1½ lbs.)
¼   tsp. salt
¼   tsp. coarsely ground pepper
3   tsp. olive oil, divided
1   large onion, chopped
1   garlic clove, minced
½   cup white wine or chicken broth
1   can (14½ oz.) diced
    tomatoes, drained
1   bay leaf
1   tsp. minced fresh rosemary or
    ¼ tsp. dried rosemary, crushed
1   tsp. minced fresh thyme or
    ¼ tsp. dried thyme
2   cans (15 oz. each) cannellini
    beans, rinsed and drained
¼   lb. smoked turkey kielbasa, chopped
3   bacon strips, cooked and crumbled

TOPPING
½   cup soft whole wheat
    bread crumbs
¼   cup minced fresh parsley
1   garlic clove, minced

1. Preheat oven to 325°. Sprinkle chicken with salt and pepper. In a broiler-safe Dutch oven, heat 2 tsp. oil over medium heat; brown chicken on both sides. Remove from the pan.

2. In same pan, saute onion in remaining oil over medium heat until crisp-tender. Add garlic; cook 1 minute. Add wine; bring to a boil, stirring to loosen browned bits from pan. Add tomatoes, herbs and chicken; return to a boil.

3. Transfer to the oven; bake, covered, for 30 minutes. Stir in the beans and kielbasa; bake, covered, until the chicken is tender, 20-25 minutes.

4. Remove from oven; preheat the broiler. Discard bay leaf; stir in bacon. Toss bread crumbs with parsley and garlic; sprinkle over top. Place in oven so surface of cassoulet is 4-5 in. from heat; broil until crumbs are golden brown, 2-3 minutes.

NOTE: To make soft bread crumbs, tear the bread into pieces and place in a food processor or blender. Cover and pulse until crumbs form. One slice of bread yields ½ to ¾ cup crumbs.

1 SERVING: 394 cal., 14g fat (4g sat. fat), 91mg chol., 736mg sod., 29g carb. (4g sugars, 8g fiber), 33g pro. **DIABETIC EXCHANGES:** 4 lean meat, 2 starch, ½ fat.

HEALTH TIP: Adding cannellini beans to a meat-based main dish bumps up the fiber and protein without adding saturated fat.

FAST FIX
CHILI HASH

Put your feet up and relax when you toss together this no-fuss dinner that always beats the clock.

—Taste of Home *Test Kitchen*

TAKES: 30 min. • **MAKES:** 4 servings

1   lb. medium potatoes, cubed
½   cup water
1   lb. ground beef
1   medium onion, chopped
1   can (15½ oz.) chili starter
1   cup frozen peas
2   Tbsp. minced fresh parsley
¼   tsp. salt
    Sour cream, optional

1. Place potatoes and water in a microwave-safe dish. Cover and microwave on high for 7 minutes or until tender.

2. Meanwhile, in a large skillet, cook beef and onion over medium heat until the meat is no longer pink; drain. Drain potatoes and add to the skillet. Stir in chili starter, peas, parsley and salt. Bring to a boil. Reduce the heat; simmer, uncovered, for 5 minutes. Serve with sour cream if desired.

1½ CUPS: 431 cal., 14g fat (5g sat. fat), 70mg chol., 1012mg sod., 45g carb. (8g sugars, 9g fiber), 29g pro.

CASSOULET FOR TODAY

DINNER POPPERS

ENCHILADA CASSER-OLÉ!

My husband loves this casserole, but it never lasts too long. Packed with black beans, cheese, tomatoes and southwest flavor, it's an impressive-looking entree that's as simple as it is simply delicious.
—*Marsha Wills, Homosassa, FL*

PREP: 25 min. • **BAKE:** 30 min.
MAKES: 8 servings

- 1 lb. lean ground beef (90% lean)
- 1 large onion, chopped
- 2 cups salsa
- 1 can (15 oz.) black beans, rinsed and drained
- ¼ cup reduced-fat Italian salad dressing
- 2 Tbsp. reduced-sodium taco seasoning
- ¼ tsp. ground cumin
- 6 flour tortillas (8 in.)
- ¾ cup reduced-fat sour cream
- 1 cup shredded reduced-fat Mexican cheese blend
- 1 cup shredded lettuce
- 1 medium tomato, chopped
- ¼ cup minced fresh cilantro

1. In a large skillet, cook beef and onion over medium heat until meat is no longer pink; drain. Stir in the salsa, beans, dressing, taco seasoning and cumin. Place three tortillas in an 11x7-in. baking dish coated with cooking spray. Layer with half of the meat mixture, sour cream and cheese. Repeat layers.
2. Cover and bake casserole at 400° for 25 minutes. Uncover; bake until heated through, 5-10 minutes longer. Let stand for 5 minutes; top with shredded lettuce, chopped tomato and cilantro.
1 PIECE: 357 cal., 12g fat (5g sat. fat), 45mg chol., 864mg sod., 37g carb. (6g sugars, 3g fiber), 23g pro. **DIABETIC EXCHANGES:** 3 lean meat, 2 starch, 1 vegetable, 1 fat.

MY TWO CENT$

"I loved this recipe. I made it for my husband's poker buddies. They gobbled it up! I will definitely make this dish again. I served it with shredded lettuce, chopped tomatoes, guacamole and extra salsa on the side."
—**CTBDE, TASTEOFHOME.COM**

---

5 INGREDIENTS

DINNER POPPERS

I could eat jalapeno poppers all day long, but who wants to say they had seven stuffed peppers for dinner? For this meal-in-one, I use poblanos for my husband and son and hotter peppers for my daughter and me.
—*Sherri Jerzyk, Tucson, AZ*

PREP: 20 min. • **BAKE:** 25 min.
MAKES: 4 servings

- 4 bacon strips
- 4 chicken tenderloins
- ¼ tsp. salt
- ⅛ tsp. pepper
- 2 tsp. canola oil
- 4 poblano peppers
- 1½ cups shredded cheddar cheese, divided
- 4 oz. cream cheese, cut into four strips

1. Preheat oven to 350°. In a large skillet, cook bacon over medium heat until partially cooked but not crisp. Remove to paper towels to drain.
2. Sprinkle chicken with salt and pepper. In a skillet, heat oil over medium-high heat; brown chicken on both sides. Cool slightly.
3. Carefully cut a slit down the side of each pepper and remove seeds. Fill each with one tenderloin; top each with 2 Tbsp. cheese and a strip of cream cheese. Close peppers; wrap with bacon and secure with toothpicks.
4. Place on a foil-lined baking sheet, slit side up. Top with remaining cheddar cheese; bake until browned and the peppers are tender, 25-30 minutes. Remove toothpicks from peppers before serving.
NOTE: Wear disposable gloves when cutting hot peppers; the oils can burn skin. Avoid touching your face.
1 STUFFED PEPPER: 389 cal., 30g fat (15g sat. fat), 96mg chol., 682mg sod., 9g carb. (4g sugars, 2g fiber), 23g pro.

ENCHILADA
CASSER-OLÉ!

FAST FIX
ONE-POT STUFFED PEPPER DINNER

With its chili-like consistency and plenty of stuffed-pepper flavor, this meal-in-one dish will warm you up on chilly days.
—*Charlotte Smith, McDonald, PA*

- -

TAKES: 30 min. • **MAKES:** 4 servings

1   lb. lean ground beef (90% lean)
3   medium green peppers, chopped (about 3 cups)
3   garlic cloves, minced
2   cans (14½ oz. each) Italian diced tomatoes, undrained
2   cups water
1   can (6 oz.) tomato paste
2   Tbsp. shredded Parmesan cheese
¼   tsp. pepper
1   cup uncooked instant rice
    Additional Parmesan cheese, optional

1. In a Dutch oven, cook and crumble the beef with the green peppers and garlic over medium-high heat until no longer pink and peppers are tender, 5-7 minutes; drain.
2. Stir in tomatoes, water, tomato paste, 2 Tbsp. cheese and pepper; bring to a boil. Stir in rice; remove from heat. Let stand, covered, 5 minutes. If desired, sprinkle with additional cheese.

2 CUPS: 415 cal., 10g fat (4g sat. fat), 72mg chol., 790mg sod., 51g carb. (20g sugars, 5g fiber), 30g pro. **DIABETIC EXCHANGES:** 3 starch, 3 lean meat.

FAST FIX | 5 INGREDIENTS
SAUSAGE-STUFFED BUTTERNUT SQUASH

Load butternut squash shells with an Italian turkey sausage and squash mixture for a quick and easy meal. Plus, it's economical and surprisingly low in calories.
—*Katia Slinger, West Jordan, UT*

- -

TAKES: 30 min. • **MAKES:** 4 servings

1   medium butternut squash (about 3 lbs.)
1   lb. Italian turkey sausage links, casings removed
1   medium onion, finely chopped
4   garlic cloves, minced
½   cup shredded Italian cheese blend
     Crushed red pepper flakes, optional

1. Preheat broiler. Cut squash lengthwise in half; discard seeds. Place squash in a large microwave-safe dish, cut side down; add ½ in. of water. Microwave, covered, on high until soft, 20-25 minutes. Cool slightly.
2. Meanwhile, in a large nonstick skillet, cook and crumble the sausage with the onion over medium-high heat until sausage is no longer pink, 5-7 minutes. Add the garlic; cook and stir 1 minute.
3. Leaving ½-in.-thick shells, scoop pulp from squash and stir into sausage mixture. Place the squash shells on a baking sheet; fill with sausage mixture. Sprinkle with the cheese.
4. Broil 4-5 in. from heat until the cheese is melted, 1-2 minutes. If desired, sprinkle with pepper flakes. To serve, cut each half into two portions.

1 SERVING: 325 cal., 10g fat (4g sat. fat), 52mg chol., 587mg sod., 44g carb. (10g sugars, 12g fiber), 19g pro. **DIABETIC EXCHANGES:** 3 starch, 3 lean meat.
HEALTH TIP: Butternut squash is an excellent source of vitamin A in the form of beta-carotene. It's important for normal vision and a healthy immune system, and it aids heart, lung and kidney function.

SAUSAGE-STUFFED BUTTERNUT SQUASH

CHICKEN OLÉ FOIL SUPPER

FAST FIX
SIRLOIN STIR-FRY WITH RAMEN NOODLES

I created this recipe when I was craving good Chinese food. The leftovers taste just as yummy when reheated the next day.
—*Annette Hemsath, Sutherlin, OR*

- -

TAKES: 30 min. • **MAKES:** 4 servings

- 2 pkg. (3 oz. each) beef ramen noodles
- 2 Tbsp. cornstarch
- 2 cups beef broth, divided
- 1 lb. beef top sirloin steak, cut into thin strips
- 2 Tbsp. canola oil
- 2 Tbsp. reduced-sodium soy sauce
- 2 cans (14 oz. each) whole baby corn, rinsed and drained
- 2 cups fresh broccoli florets
- 1 cup diced sweet red pepper
- 1 cup shredded carrots
- 4 green onions, cut into 1-in. pieces
- ½ cup unsalted peanuts

1. Set aside seasoning packets from the noodles. Cook the noodles according to package directions.
2. Meanwhile, in a small bowl, combine the cornstarch and ¼ cup broth until smooth; set aside. In a large skillet or wok, stir-fry beef in oil until no longer pink. Add the soy sauce; cook until the liquid has evaporated, 3-4 minutes. Remove beef and keep warm.
3. Add the baby corn, broccoli, red pepper, carrots, onions and remaining broth to the pan. Sprinkle with contents of seasoning packets. Stir-fry until the vegetables are crisp-tender, 5-7 minutes.
4. Stir the cornstarch mixture and add to the skillet. Bring to a boil; cook and stir until thickened, about 2 minutes. Drain noodles. Add beef and noodles to pan; heat through. Garnish with peanuts.

1½ CUPS: 593 cal., 28g fat (8g sat. fat), 46mg chol., 2022mg sod., 49g carb. (8g sugars, 8g fiber), 38g pro.

FAST FIX
CHICKEN OLÉ FOIL SUPPER

These Mexi-style chicken packets can be assembled ahead and frozen if you like. Just thaw them overnight in the fridge, then grill as directed. I like to serve them with warm tortillas and fresh fruit on the side.
—*Mary Peck, Salina, KS*

- -

TAKES: 30 min. • **MAKES:** 4 servings

- 1 can (15 oz.) black beans, rinsed and drained
- 2 cups fresh or frozen corn (about 10 oz.), thawed
- 1 cup salsa
- 4 boneless skinless chicken breast halves (4 oz. each)
- ¼ tsp. garlic powder
- ¼ tsp. pepper
- ⅛ tsp. salt
- 1 cup shredded cheddar cheese
- 2 green onions, chopped

1. Mix beans, corn and salsa; divide among four 18x12-in. pieces of heavy-duty foil. Top with chicken. Mix seasonings; sprinkle over chicken. Fold foil over chicken, sealing tightly.
2. Grill packets, covered, over medium heat until a thermometer inserted in the chicken reads 165°, 15-20 minutes. Open the foil carefully to allow steam to escape. Sprinkle with cheese and green onions.

1 PACKET: 405 cal., 13g fat (6g sat. fat), 91mg chol., 766mg sod., 34g carb. (8g sugars, 6g fiber), 37g pro. **DIABETIC EXCHANGES:** 4 lean meat, 2 starch, 1 fat.

BEER PORK CHOPS

AFFORDABLE ENTREES: PORK, SEAFOOD & MEATLESS

You'll find even more satisfying main courses in this unbeatable chapter.
Best of all, they each keep grocery bills in check. The 28 recipes that follow offer
full-flavored comfort, taking pork, fish and seafood dishes to new heights.
You'll also discover a few meatless options for change-of-pace dinners.

BEER PORK CHOPS

These tender chops in a savory sauce are perfect for a hectic weeknight because they're so easy to prepare. They use only a handful of ingredients! Try them with hot buttered noodles.

—*Jana Christian, Farson, WY*

TAKES: 20 min. • **MAKES:** 4 servings

- 4 boneless pork loin chops (4 oz. each)
- ½ tsp. salt
- ½ tsp. pepper
- 1 Tbsp. canola oil
- 3 Tbsp. ketchup
- 2 Tbsp. brown sugar
- ¾ cup beer or nonalcoholic beer

1. Sprinkle pork chops with salt and pepper. In a large skillet, heat oil over medium heat; brown chops on both sides.

2. Mix ketchup, brown sugar and beer; pour over the chops. Bring to a boil. Reduce heat; simmer, uncovered, until a thermometer inserted in pork reads 145°, 4-6 minutes. Let stand 5 minutes before serving.

FREEZE OPTION: Place the pork chops in freezer containers; top with sauce. Cool and freeze. To use, partially thaw pork chops in the refrigerator overnight. Heat through in a covered saucepan, gently stirring sauce and adding a little water if necessary.

1 PORK CHOP: 239 cal., 10g fat (3g sat. fat), 55mg chol., 472mg sod., 11g carb. (11g sugars, 0 fiber), 22g pro. **DIABETIC EXCHANGES:** 3 lean meat, 1 fat, ½ starch.

MY TWO CENT$

"I made this for dinner tonight, and it was awesome. I doubled the sauce because I wanted to use up the beer. My hubby loved it. I think it would also be good with chicken breast. Will definitely use this recipe again."

—BASKITMUM1, TASTEOFHOME.COM

PESTO CORN SALAD WITH SHRIMP

PESTO CORN SALAD WITH SHRIMP

Showcase summer flavor with fresh corn, tomatoes and basil in this delicious salad. If you make it a day early, spritz the salad with lemon juice before covering and putting it in the fridge to prevent browning.

—*Deena Bowen, Chico, CA*

TAKES: 30 min. • **MAKES:** 4 servings

- 4 medium ears sweet corn, husked
- ½ cup packed fresh basil leaves
- ¼ cup olive oil
- ½ tsp. salt, divided
- 1½ cups cherry tomatoes, halved
- ⅛ tsp. pepper
- 1 medium ripe avocado, peeled and chopped
- 1 lb. uncooked shrimp (31-40 per lb.), peeled and deveined

1. In a pot of boiling water, cook corn until tender, about 5 minutes. Drain; cool slightly. Meanwhile, in a food processor, pulse basil, oil and ¼ tsp. salt until blended.

2. Cut corn from cob and place in a bowl. Stir in tomatoes, pepper and remaining salt. Add the avocado and 2 Tbsp. basil mixture; toss gently to combine.

3. Thread the shrimp onto metal or soaked wooden skewers; brush with remaining basil mixture. Grill, covered, over medium heat until shrimp turn pink, 2-4 minutes per side. Remove shrimp from skewers; serve with corn mixture.

1 SERVING: 371 cal., 22g fat (3g sat. fat), 138mg chol., 450mg sod., 25g carb. (8g sugars, 5g fiber), 23g pro.

TORTELLINI
CARBONARA

TORTELLINI CARBONARA

Bacon, cream and Parmesan cheese make a classic pasta sauce that's absolutely heavenly. It's a great option for company that's easy on the wallet.
—*Cathy Croyle, Davidsville, PA*

TAKES: 20 min. • **MAKES:** 4 servings

- 1 pkg. (9 oz.) refrigerated cheese tortellini
- 8 bacon strips, chopped
- 1 cup heavy whipping cream
- ½ cup grated Parmesan cheese
- ½ cup chopped fresh parsley

1. Cook tortellini according to the package directions; drain.
2. Meanwhile, in a large skillet, cook the bacon over medium heat until crisp, stirring occasionally. Remove with a slotted spoon; drain on paper towels. Pour off drippings.
3. In same pan, combine cream, Parmesan cheese, parsley and bacon; heat through over medium heat. Stir in tortellini.
1 CUP: 527 cal., 36g fat (20g sat. fat), 121mg chol., 728mg sod., 33g carb. (3g sugars, 2g fiber), 19g pro.

OUR TWO CENT$

- Traditional carbonara often has egg in the sauce. If you'd like to give it a try, consider halving the cream and tempering two whisked eggs into the sauce.
- Temper eggs by adding a small amount of the hot mixture to the whisked egg before adding it all back to the pan. Be sure to do this after removing pan from the heat to keep the eggs from scrambling.

SKILLET HAM & RICE

FAST FIX

SKILLET HAM & RICE

This homey stovetop dish features a tasty combination of ham, rice and mushrooms. And it's ready in just 25 minutes.
—*Susan Zivec, Regina, SK*

TAKES: 25 min. • **MAKES:** 2 servings

- 1 tsp. olive oil
- 1 medium onion, chopped
- 1 cup sliced fresh mushrooms
- 1 cup cubed fully cooked ham
- ⅛ tsp. pepper
- ½ cup reduced-sodium chicken broth
- ¼ cup water
- ¾ cup uncooked instant rice
- 2 green onions, sliced
- ¼ cup shredded Parmesan cheese

1. In a large nonstick skillet, heat oil over medium-high heat; saute the onion and mushrooms until tender. Stir in the ham, pepper, broth and water; bring to a boil. Stir in rice. Reduce heat; simmer, covered, until rice is tender, about 5 minutes.
2. Fluff with a fork. Top with green onions and cheese.
1¼ CUPS: 322 cal., 8g fat (3g sat. fat), 49mg chol., 1168mg sod., 38g carb. (4g sugars, 2g fiber), 24g pro.
HEALTH TIP: You will find lower-sodium varieties of ham in the meat and deli sections. They typically have 25 to 30 percent less sodium than other versions.

ITALIAN-STYLE PORK CHOPS

In the early years of my marriage, this recipe for Italian-style pork chops was one of the first I tried making. Over the years, I've made it a bit healthier by reducing the oil and fat and by adding some vegetables. It's excellent over hot rice.
—*Traci Hoppes, Spring Valley, CA*

TAKES: 30 min. • **MAKES:** 4 servings

- 2 medium green peppers, cut into ¼-in. strips
- ½ lb. sliced fresh mushrooms
- 1 Tbsp. plus 1½ tsp. olive oil, divided
- 4 boneless pork loin chops (6 oz. each)
- ¾ tsp. salt, divided
- ¾ tsp. pepper, divided
- 2 cups marinara or spaghetti sauce
- 1 can (3½ oz.) sliced ripe olives, drained

1. In a large skillet, saute peppers and mushrooms in 1 Tbsp. oil until tender. Remove and keep warm.
2. Sprinkle chops with ¼ tsp. salt and ¼ tsp. pepper. In the same skillet, brown chops in remaining oil. Add the marinara sauce, olives, the remaining salt and pepper, and reserved pepper mixture. Bring to a boil. Reduce heat; cover and simmer until a thermometer inserted in pork reads 145°, 10-15 minutes. Let stand for 5 minutes before serving.

1 PORK CHOP WITH ¾ CUP SAUCE: 397 cal., 18g fat (5g sat. fat), 82mg chol., 930mg sod., 22g carb. (12g sugars, 5g fiber), 37g pro.

OUR TWO CENT$

If you have canned mushrooms on hand, go ahead and use them for this dish instead of the fresh.

SPINACH & GOUDA-STUFFED PORK CUTLETS

JOAN OAKLAND
Troy, MT

SPINACH & GOUDA-STUFFED PORK CUTLETS

This started as a restaurant copycat dish at home. Cheese just oozes out of the center, and mustard lends a lot of flavor.
—*Joan Oakland, Troy, MT*

TAKES: 30 min. • **MAKES:** 2 servings

- 3 Tbsp. dry bread crumbs
- 2 Tbsp. grated Parmesan cheese
- 2 pork sirloin cutlets (3 oz. each)
- ¼ tsp. salt
- ⅛ tsp. pepper
- 2 slices smoked Gouda cheese (about 2 oz.)
- 2 cups fresh baby spinach
- 2 Tbsp. horseradish mustard

1. Preheat oven to 400°. In a shallow bowl, mix bread crumbs and Parmesan cheese.
2. Sprinkle tops of cutlets with salt and pepper. Layer one end of each with Gouda cheese and spinach. Fold cutlets in half, enclosing filling; secure with toothpicks. Brush mustard over outsides of pork; dip in bread crumb mixture, patting to help coating adhere.
3. Place cutlets on a greased foil-lined baking sheet. Bake until golden brown and pork is tender, 12-15 minutes. Discard toothpicks before serving.

1 STUFFED CUTLET: 299 cal., 16g fat (7g sat. fat), 91mg chol., 898mg sod., 10g carb. (2g sugars, 2g fiber), 30g pro.

SUMMER CARBONARA

Basil and bacon make the best summer buds in this smoky-sweet pasta. I like to serve it with a simple spring mix salad dressed in balsamic, and a good Chardonnay wine or a glass of cold iced tea.

—Cathy Dudderar, Lexington, KY

- -

PREP: 20 min. • **COOK:** 15 min.
MAKES: 6 servings

- 1 pkg. (16 oz.) spaghetti
- 2 Tbsp. olive oil
- 1 large sweet onion, finely chopped
- 1 medium yellow summer squash, diced
- 1 medium zucchini, diced
- 2 garlic cloves, minced
- 4 plum tomatoes, seeded and chopped
- 2 large eggs, lightly beaten
- 1 cup grated Parmesan cheese
- 12 bacon strips, cooked and crumbled
- ¼ cup fresh basil leaves, thinly sliced
- 1 tsp. minced fresh oregano
- ½ tsp. salt
- ¼ tsp. pepper

1. Cook spaghetti according to package directions. Drain; transfer to a large bowl.
2. Meanwhile, in a large skillet, heat oil over medium-high heat. Add the onion, squash, zucchini and garlic; cook and stir until tender. Add tomatoes; heat through. Remove from pan; keep warm.
3. Reduce heat to low. Add eggs to same skillet; cook slowly, stirring constantly, until eggs reach 160° and just begin to coat a metal spoon (eggs will be frothy; do not overcook). Add to hot spaghetti; toss to coat. Add vegetables and the remaining ingredients; toss gently to combine.

1½ CUPS: 508 cal., 17g fat (5g sat. fat), 96mg chol., 732mg sod., 66g carb. (7g sugars, 4g fiber), 23g pro.

FAST FIX

CREAMY PAPRIKA PORK

When I was little, I would often ask my mom to make "my favorite meat." She knew what I was really requesting was this homey pork recipe. It's been in my family for more than 30 years and it's still a hit!

—Alexandra Barnett, Forest, VA

- -

TAKES: 30 min. • **MAKES:** 4 servings

- 1 pork tenderloin (1 lb.), cut into 1-in. cubes
- 1 tsp. all-purpose flour
- 4 tsp. paprika
- ¾ tsp. salt
- ¼ tsp. pepper
- 1 Tbsp. butter
- ¾ cup heavy whipping cream
  Hot cooked egg noodles or rice
  Minced fresh parsley, optional

1. Toss pork with flour and seasonings. In a large skillet, heat the butter over medium heat; saute the pork until lightly browned, 4-5 minutes.
2. Add the cream; bring to a boil, stirring to loosen the browned bits from pan. Cook, uncovered, until cream is slightly thickened, 5-7 minutes.
3. Serve with noodles. If desired, sprinkle with parsley.

¾ CUP PORK MIXTURE: 320 cal., 23g fat (14g sat. fat), 122mg chol., 524mg sod., 3g carb. (1g sugars, 1g fiber), 24g pro.

SUMMER CARBONARA

BLACKENED TILAPIA WITH
ZUCCHINI NOODLES

5 INGREDIENTS

BACON-WRAPPED PESTO PORK TENDERLOIN

I love to serve this family-favorite pork tenderloin—maybe because of all the compliments that come with it! When the weather warms up, we grill it instead.
—*Megan Riofski, Frankfort, IL*

PREP: 30 min. • **BAKE:** 20 min.
MAKES: 4 servings

10 bacon strips
1 pork tenderloin (1 lb.)
¼ tsp. pepper
⅓ cup prepared pesto
1 cup shredded Italian cheese blend
1 cup fresh baby spinach

1. Preheat oven to 425°. Arrange bacon strips lengthwise in a foil-lined 15x10x1-in. pan, overlapping slightly.
2. Cut the tenderloin lengthwise through the center to within ½ in. of bottom. Open the tenderloin flat; cover with plastic wrap. Pound with a meat mallet to ½-in. thickness. Remove plastic; place tenderloin on center of bacon, perpendicular to strips.
3. Sprinkle pepper over pork. Spread with pesto; layer with cheese and spinach. Close tenderloin; wrap with bacon, overlapping ends. Tie with kitchen string at 3-in. intervals. Secure ends with toothpicks.
4. In a 12-in. skillet, brown roast on all sides, about 8 minutes. Return to baking pan; roast in oven until a thermometer inserted in the pork reads 145°, 17-20 minutes. Remove string and toothpicks; let stand 5 minutes before slicing.
1 SERVING: 402 cal., 25g fat (9g sat. fat), 104mg chol., 864mg sod., 4g carb. (1g sugars, 1g fiber), 37g pro.

FAST FIX

BLACKENED TILAPIA WITH ZUCCHINI NOODLES

I love quick and bright meals like this one-skillet wonder. Homemade pico de gallo is easy to make the night before.
—*Tammy Brownlow, Dallas, TX*

TAKES: 30 min. • **MAKES:** 4 servings

2 large zucchini (about 1½ lbs.)
1½ tsp. ground cumin
¾ tsp. salt, divided
½ tsp. smoked paprika
½ tsp. pepper
¼ tsp garlic powder
4 tilapia fillets (6 oz. each)
2 tsp. olive oil
2 garlic cloves, minced
1 cup pico de gallo

1. Trim ends of zucchini. Using a spiralizer, cut zucchini into thin strands.
2. Mix cumin, ½ tsp. salt, paprika, pepper and garlic powder; sprinkle generously onto both sides of the tilapia. In a large nonstick skillet, heat oil over medium-high heat. In batches, cook tilapia until fish just begins to flake easily with a fork, 2-3 minutes per side. Remove from pan; keep fish warm.
3. In same pan, cook zucchini with garlic over medium-high heat until slightly softened, 1-2 minutes, tossing constantly with tongs (do not overcook). Sprinkle with remaining salt. Serve with tilapia and pico de gallo.
NOTE: If you don't have a spiralizer, zucchini may be cut into ribbons with a vegetable peeler. Saute as directed, increasing the time as necessary.
1 SERVING: 203 cal., 4g fat (1g sat. fat), 83mg chol., 522mg sod., 8g carb. (5g sugars, 2g fiber), 34g pro. **DIABETIC EXCHANGES:** 5 lean meat, 1 vegetable, ½ fat.

BACON-WRAPPED PESTO PORK TENDERLOIN

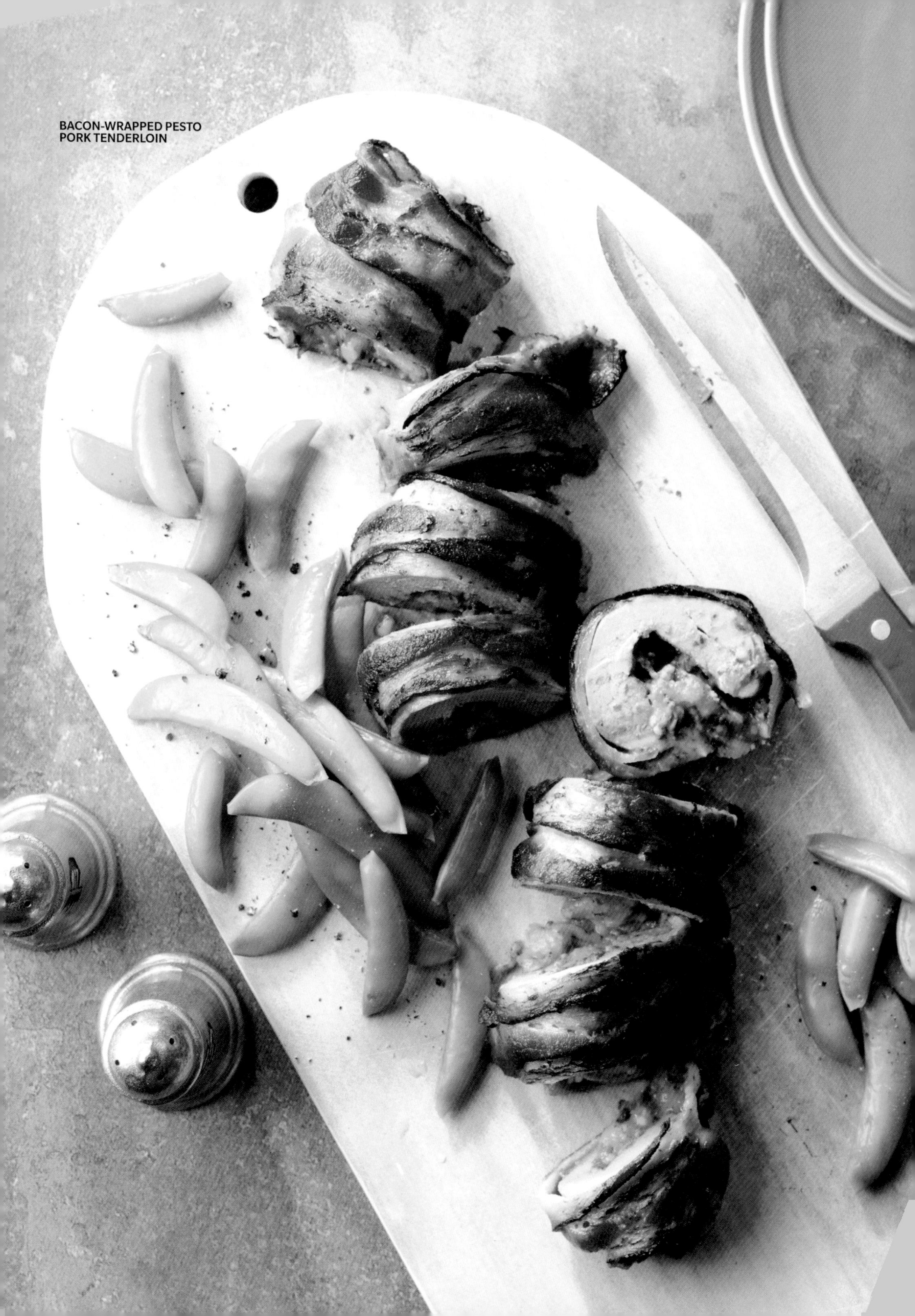

SPICY SHRIMP & PENNE PASTA

I created this creamy pasta dish because I needed to use up some marinara. The red pepper flakes give it a little heat, which my family loves. It's super versatile, so try it with chicken or stir in some fresh basil.
—*Lorri Stout, Gaithersburg, MD*

TAKES: 30 min. • **MAKES:** 6 servings

- 3 cups uncooked penne pasta (about 12 oz.)
- 1 Tbsp. butter, divided
- 1 Tbsp. olive oil, divided
- 2 lbs. uncooked shrimp (31-40 per lb.), peeled and deveined, divided
- ½ tsp. crushed red pepper flakes, divided
- 1 jar (24 oz.) marinara sauce
- ¾ cup half-and-half cream
- 4 cups chopped fresh spinach

1. In a 6-qt. stockpot, cook the penne pasta according to package directions; drain and return to pot.
2. In a large skillet, heat half of the butter and half of the oil over medium-high heat. Saute half of the shrimp with ¼ tsp. pepper flakes until shrimp turn pink, 3-5 minutes; remove from pan. Repeat.
3. In same pan, heat the marinara sauce and cream just to a boil over medium heat, stirring to blend. Stir in spinach until wilted; add to pasta. Stir in shrimp; heat through.

1⅔ CUPS: 395 cal., 12g fat (4g sat. fat), 206mg chol., 702mg sod., 38g carb. (9g sugars, 4g fiber), 33g pro. **DIABETIC EXCHANGES:** 4 lean meat, 2 starch, 1 vegetable, 1 fat.

JUST PEACHY PORK TENDERLOIN

I had a pork tenderloin and ripe peaches and decided to put them together. The results couldn't have been more irresistible! It's a fresh entree that tastes like summer.
—*Julia Gosliga, Addison, VT*

TAKES: 20 min. • **MAKES:** 4 servings

- 1 lb. pork tenderloin, cut into 12 slices
- ½ tsp. salt
- ¼ tsp. pepper
- 2 tsp. olive oil
- 4 medium peaches, peeled and sliced
- 1 Tbsp. lemon juice
- ¼ cup peach preserves

1. Flatten each tenderloin slice to ¼-in. thickness. Sprinkle with salt and pepper. In a large nonstick skillet over medium heat, cook tenderloin in oil until tender. Remove and keep warm.
2. Add peaches and lemon juice, stirring to loosen browned bits from pan. Cook and stir until peaches are tender, 3-4 minutes. Stir in the pork and preserves; heat through.

1 SERVING: 241 cal., 6g fat (2g sat. fat), 63mg chol., 340mg sod., 23g carb. (20g sugars, 2g fiber), 23g pro. **DIABETIC EXCHANGES:** 3 lean meat, 1 fruit, ½ starch, ½ fat.

SPICY SHRIMP & PENNE PASTA

CHEESE TORTELLINI WITH TOMATOES & CORN

FAST FIX

CHEESE TORTELLINI WITH TOMATOES & CORN

Fresh corn and basil make this meatless entree a great option for casual outdoor dining. Try it alongside any entree for a side dish, too!
—*Sally Maloney, Dallas, GA*

- -

TAKES: 25 min. • **MAKES:** 4 servings

- 1 pkg. (9 oz.) refrigerated cheese tortellini
- 3⅓ cups fresh or frozen corn (about 16 oz.)
- 2 cups cherry tomatoes, quartered
- 2 green onions, thinly sliced
- ¼ cup minced fresh basil
- 2 Tbsp. grated Parmesan cheese
- 4 tsp. olive oil
- ¼ tsp. garlic powder
- ⅛ tsp. pepper

In a 6-qt. stockpot, cook tortellini according to package directions, adding corn during the last 5 minutes of cooking. Drain; transfer to a large bowl. Add remaining ingredients; toss to coat.

1¾ CUPS: 366 cal., 12g fat (4g sat. fat), 30mg chol., 286mg sod., 57g carb. (6g sugars, 5g fiber), 14g pro.

FAST FIX | 5 INGREDIENTS

CITRUS-SPICE GLAZED SALMON

Got 5 minutes? Then you've got the time to get these fillets into the oven. They're perfect for entertaining, yet simple enough for family weeknight dinners.
—*Karen Latimer, Winnipeg, MB*

- -

TAKES: 20 min. • **MAKES:** 4 servings

- 4 salmon fillets (6 oz. each)
- 2 Tbsp. orange marmalade
- 1 tsp. reduced-sodium soy sauce
- ¼ tsp. Chinese five-spice powder
- ⅛ tsp. salt
- ⅛ tsp. ground ginger

1. Line a baking sheet with foil; grease foil. Place salmon on the baking sheet.
2. Place marmalade in a small microwave-safe bowl. Microwave until warmed, about 10 seconds. Stir in the soy sauce, five-spice powder, salt and ginger. Spoon over salmon.
3. Bake, uncovered, at 350° until fish flakes easily with a fork, 15-20 minutes.

1 FILLET: 291 cal., 16g fat (3g sat. fat), 85mg chol., 215mg sod., 7g carb. (6g sugars, 0 fiber), 29g pro. **DIABETIC EXCHANGES:** 5 lean meat, ½ starch.

FAST FIX

SALSA BLACK BEAN BURGERS

Meatless meals get a thumbs-up rating when these hearty bean burgers are on the menu. Guacamole and sour cream make them seem decadent.
—*Jill Reichardt, Saint Louis, MO*

- -

TAKES: 30 min. • **MAKES:** 4 servings

- 1 can (15 oz.) black beans, rinsed and drained
- ⅔ cup dry bread crumbs
- 1 small tomato, seeded and finely chopped
- 1 jalapeno pepper, seeded and finely chopped
- 1 large egg
- 1 tsp. minced fresh cilantro
- 1 garlic clove, minced
- 1 Tbsp. olive oil
- 4 whole wheat hamburger buns, split Reduced-fat sour cream and guacamole, optional

1. Place beans in a food processor; cover and process until blended. Transfer to a large bowl. Add the bread crumbs, tomato, jalapeno, egg, cilantro and garlic. Mix until combined. Shape into four patties.
2. In a large nonstick skillet, cook patties in oil in batches over medium heat until lightly browned, 4-6 minutes on each side. Serve on buns. If desired, top with reduced-fat sour cream and guacamole.
NOTE: Wear disposable gloves when cutting hot peppers; the oils can burn skin. Avoid touching your face.
1 BURGER: 323 cal., 8g fat (1g sat. fat), 53mg chol., 557mg sod., 51g carb. (6g sugars, 9g fiber), 13g pro.

MY TWO CENT$

"I love how quickly these burgers come together. I skipped the jalapeno and cilantro, and I added salsa instead of a tomato. I served them with some red onion on top and sweet potato fries on the side."
—HKPEPIN, TASTEOFHOME.COM

**BLACK BEAN & SWEET
POTATO RICE BOWLS**

KIM VAN DUNK
Caldwell, NJ

BLACK BEAN & SWEET POTATO RICE BOWLS

With three hungry boys in my house, dinners need to be quick and filling, and it helps to get in some veggies, too. This one is a favorite because it's hearty, and I can easily tweak it with different ingredients.
—*Kim Van Dunk, Caldwell, NJ*

TAKES: 30 min. • **MAKES:** 4 servings

- ¾ cup uncooked long grain rice
- ¼ tsp. garlic salt
- 1½ cups water
- 3 Tbsp. olive oil, divided
- 1 large sweet potato, peeled and diced
- 1 medium red onion, finely chopped
- 4 cups chopped fresh kale (tough stems removed)
- 1 can (15 oz.) black beans, rinsed and drained
- 2 Tbsp. sweet chili sauce
  Lime wedges, optional
  Additional sweet chili sauce, optional

1. Place rice, garlic salt and water in a large saucepan; bring to a boil. Reduce the heat; simmer, covered, until water is absorbed and rice is tender, 15-20 minutes. Remove from heat; let stand 5 minutes.
2. Meanwhile, in a large skillet, heat 2 Tbsp. oil over medium-high heat; saute the sweet potato 8 minutes. Add onion; cook and stir until potato is tender, 4-6 minutes. Add kale; cook and stir until tender, 3-5 minutes. Stir in beans; heat through.
3. Gently stir 2 Tbsp. chili sauce and the remaining oil into rice; add to the potato mixture. If desired, serve with lime wedges and additional chili sauce.
2 CUPS: 435 cal., 11g fat (2g sat. fat), 0 chol., 405mg sod., 74g carb. (15g sugars, 8g fiber), 10g pro.
HEALTH TIP: Sweet potato + kale + black beans = nearly ⅓ of the daily value for fiber per serving!

SAUSAGE & SPINACH CALZONES

FAST FIX | 5 INGREDIENTS

SAUSAGE & SPINACH CALZONES

These comforting calzones are perfect for quick meals—or even a midnight snack. My co-workers ask me to make these when it's my turn to bring in lunch.
—*Kourtney Williams, Mechanicsville, VA*

TAKES: 30 min. • **MAKES:** 4 servings

- ½ lb. bulk Italian sausage
- 3 cups fresh baby spinach
- 1 tube (13.8 oz.) refrigerated pizza crust
- ¾ cup shredded part-skim mozzarella cheese
- ½ cup part-skim ricotta cheese
- ¼ tsp. pepper
  Pizza sauce, optional

1. Preheat oven to 400°. In a large skillet, cook and crumble sausage over medium heat until no longer pink, 4-6 minutes; drain. Add the spinach; cook and stir until wilted. Remove from heat.
2. On a lightly floured surface, unroll and pat dough into a 15x11-in. rectangle. Cut into four rectangles. Sprinkle mozzarella cheese on one half of each rectangle to within 1 in. of edges.
3. Stir ricotta cheese and pepper into sausage mixture; spoon over mozzarella cheese. Fold the dough over filling; press edges with a fork to seal. Place on a greased baking sheet.
4. Bake calzones until light golden brown, 10-15 minutes. If desired, serve calzones with pizza sauce.
FREEZE OPTION: Freeze cooled calzones in a freezer container. To use, microwave on high until heated through.
1 CALZONE: 489 cal., 22g fat (9g sat. fat), 54mg chol., 1242mg sod., 51g carb. (7g sugars, 2g fiber), 23g pro.

BASIL POLENTA WITH RATATOUILLE

For our wedding reception, we wanted to provide a vegan menu to our guests. Everyone raved about this polenta topped with colorful ratatouille—our version of the classic stewed vegetable dish.
—*Kimberly Hammond, Kingwood, TX*

PREP: 25 min. + chilling • **COOK:** 40 min.
MAKES: 4 servings

4   cups water
½   tsp. salt, divided
1   cup cornmeal
½   cup minced fresh basil
1   medium eggplant, peeled and cut into ½-in. cubes
1   medium onion, halved and sliced
1   medium green pepper, julienned
5   Tbsp. olive oil, divided
4   garlic cloves, minced
1   can (14½ oz.) diced tomatoes, drained
½   cup pitted Greek olives, sliced
1   tsp. dried oregano
¼   tsp. pepper
     Fresh basil leaves

1. In a large heavy saucepan, bring water and ¼ tsp. salt to a boil. Reduce heat to a gentle boil; slowly whisk in cornmeal. Cook and stir with a wooden spoon until the polenta is thickened and pulls away cleanly from the sides of the pan, 15-20 minutes. Stir in basil.
2. Spread into an 8-in. square baking dish coated with cooking spray. Refrigerate for 30 minutes.
3. Meanwhile, in a large skillet, saute the eggplant, onion and green pepper in 2 Tbsp. oil until crisp-tender. Add the garlic; cook 1 minute longer. Stir in the tomatoes, olives, oregano, pepper and remaining salt. Cook and stir over medium heat until vegetables are tender, 10-12 minutes.
4. Cut polenta into four squares. In another large skillet, cook polenta in remaining oil in batches until golden brown, 7-8 minutes on each side. Serve with the ratatouille; garnish with basil.
1 POLENTA SQUARE WITH 1 CUP RATATOUILLE: 400 cal., 22g fat (3g sat. fat), 0 chol., 709mg sod., 46g carb. (9g sugars, 10g fiber), 6g pro.

GARLIC LEMON SHRIMP

FAST FIX
GARLIC LEMON SHRIMP

This shrimp dish is amazingly quick. Serve it with crusty bread so you can soak up the luscious garlic lemon sauce.
—*Athena Russell, Greenville, SC*

TAKES: 20 min. • **MAKES:** 4 servings

2   Tbsp. olive oil
1   lb. uncooked shrimp (26-30 per lb.), peeled and deveined
3   garlic cloves, thinly sliced
1   Tbsp. lemon juice
1   tsp. ground cumin
¼   tsp. salt
2   Tbsp. minced fresh parsley
     Hot cooked pasta or rice

In a large skillet, heat oil over medium-high heat; saute shrimp 3 minutes. Add garlic, lemon juice, cumin and salt; cook and stir until shrimp turn pink. Stir in parsley. Serve with pasta.
1 SERVING: 163 cal., 8g fat (1g sat. fat), 138mg chol., 284mg sod., 2g carb. (0 sugars, 0 fiber), 19g pro. **DIABETIC EXCHANGES:** 3 lean meat, 1½ fat.

HEALTH TIP: Cooking the shrimp in olive oil instead of butter saves about 3 grams of saturated fat per serving.

BROILED COD

This is the easiest and tastiest fish you'll serve. Even finicky eaters who think they don't like fish will love the beautiful and flaky results.

—Kim Russell, North Wales, PA

- -

TAKES: 30 min. • **MAKES:** 2 servings

- ¼ cup fat-free Italian salad dressing
- ½ tsp. sugar
- ⅛ tsp. salt
- ⅛ tsp. garlic powder
- ⅛ tsp. curry powder
- ⅛ tsp. paprika
- ⅛ tsp. pepper
- 2 cod fillets (6 oz. each)
- 2 tsp. butter

1. Preheat broiler. In a shallow bowl, mix first seven ingredients; add cod, turning to coat. Let stand 10-15 minutes.

2. Place fillets on a greased rack of a broiler pan; discard the remaining marinade. Broil 3-4 in. from heat until the fish just begins to flake easily with a fork, 10-12 minutes. Top with butter.

1 FILLET: 168 cal., 5g fat (3g sat. fat), 75mg chol., 365mg sod., 2g carb. (2g sugars, 0 fiber), 27g pro. **DIABETIC EXCHANGES:** 4 lean meat, 1 fat.

FAST FIX | 5 INGREDIENTS

PINEAPPLE CRANBERRY HAM

Tired of the same old meals for dinner? Try something new tonight! A sweet and tangy relish of cranberries and pineapple tops these hearty ham steaks, adding lots of flavor and color.

—Rita Brower, Exeter, CA

- -

TAKES: 25 min. • **MAKES:** 4 servings

- 4 boneless fully cooked ham steaks (6 oz. each)
- 1½ tsp. canola oil
- ½ cup jellied cranberry sauce
- ½ cup undrained crushed pineapple
- 3 Tbsp. brown sugar
- ⅛ tsp. ground cloves

1. Cut each ham steak in half. In a large skillet over medium heat, cook the ham in oil in batches until browned and heated through, 3-5 minutes on each side. Set ham aside and keep warm.

2. Meanwhile, in a small saucepan, mash the cranberry sauce; stir in the remaining ingredients. Bring to a boil; cook and stir until slightly thickened, 3-5 minutes. Serve with ham.

1 SERVING: 405 cal., 16g fat (5g sat. fat), 90mg chol., 2186mg sod., 33g carb. (25g sugars, 1g fiber), 31g pro.

FAST FIX

CAJUN PECAN CATFISH

Instead of dredging the catfish to bread it, I just sprinkle the seasonings over the top. It's just as crunchy, but without the mess. I serve it with biscuits and mixed fruit.

—Jan Wilkins, Blytheville, AR

- -

TAKES: 25 min. • **MAKES:** 4 servings

- 2 Tbsp. olive oil
- 2 tsp. lemon juice
- 1 tsp. Cajun seasoning
- ½ tsp. dried thyme
- ⅓ cup finely chopped pecans
- 2 Tbsp. grated Parmesan cheese
- 1 Tbsp. dry bread crumbs
- 1 Tbsp. dried parsley flakes
- 4 catfish fillets (6 oz. each)

1. Preheat oven to 425°. In a small bowl, combine oil, lemon juice, Cajun seasoning and thyme. In another bowl, combine the pecans, cheese, bread crumbs, parsley and 1 Tbsp. of the oil mixture.

2. Place the catfish in a greased 15x10x1-in. baking pan. Brush with remaining oil mixture. Spread pecan mixture over fillets. Bake until fish flakes easily with a fork, 10-15 minutes.

1 FILLET: 377 cal., 28g fat (5g sat. fat), 82mg chol., 277mg sod., 3g carb. (1g sugars, 1g fiber), 29g pro.

BROILED COD

PEPPERED
PORK PITAS

SLOW COOKER
SLOW-COOKER MAC & CHEESE

This classic casserole is a rich and cheesy meatless main dish. I've never met anyone who didn't ask for second helpings.
—*Bernice Glascoe, Roxboro, NC*

PREP: 15 min. • **COOK:** 3¾ hours
MAKES: 10 servings

- 1   pkg. (16 oz.) elbow macaroni
- ½   cup butter, melted
- 4   cups shredded cheddar cheese, divided
- 1   can (12 oz.) evaporated milk
- 1   can (10¾ oz.) condensed cheddar cheese soup, undiluted
- 1   cup 2% milk
- 2   large eggs, beaten
- ⅛   tsp. paprika

1. Cook macaroni according to package directions; drain. Place in a 5-qt. slow cooker; add the butter. In a large bowl, mix 3 cups cheese, evaporated milk, condensed soup, 2% milk and eggs. Pour over macaroni mixture; stir to combine. Cook, covered, on low 3½-4 hours or until a thermometer reads at least 160°.
2. Sprinkle with remaining cheese. Cook, covered, on low until the cheese is melted, 15-20 minutes longer. Sprinkle with paprika.
1 SERVING: 502 cal., 28g fat (18g sat. fat), 131mg chol., 638mg sod., 42g carb. (7g sugars, 2g fiber), 21g pro.

OUR TWO CENT$
Frugal cooks are always on the lookout to use up leftovers. Have some grilled chicken in the fridge? What about last night's Sloppy Joe filling? Stir in cooked meats during the last 20 minutes of cooking time for an amped-up meal.

FAST FIX | 5 INGREDIENTS
PEPPERED PORK PITAS

Cracked black pepper is all it takes to give my pork pitas some pop. The pitas make any weeknight meal or workday lunch a special experience. I especially like to fill them up with caramelized onions and garlic mayo.
—*Katherine White, Henderson, NV*

TAKES: 20 min. • **MAKES:** 4 servings

- 1   lb. boneless pork loin chops, cut into thin strips
- 1   Tbsp. olive oil
- 2   tsp. coarsely ground pepper
- 2   garlic cloves, minced
- 1   jar (12 oz.) roasted sweet red peppers, drained and julienned
- 4   whole pita breads, warmed
     Garlic mayonnaise and torn leaf lettuce, optional

In a small bowl, combine pork, oil, pepper and garlic; toss to coat. Place a large skillet over medium-high heat. Add pork mixture; cook and stir until no longer pink. Stir in red peppers; heat through. Serve on pita breads. Top with mayonnaise and lettuce if desired.
1 PITA: 380 cal., 11g fat (3g sat. fat), 55mg chol., 665mg sod., 37g carb. (4g sugars, 2g fiber), 27g pro. **DIABETIC EXCHANGES:** 3 lean meat, 2 starch, 1 fat.

**SLOW-COOKER
MAC & CHEESE**

CURRIED SHRIMP PASTA

This light and spicy shrimp dish comes together easily. My favorite pasta to use is angel hair, but spaghetti works fine if that's what you have on hand.
—*Thomas Faglon, Somerset, NJ*

TAKES: 25 min. • **MAKES:** 4 servings

- 8 oz. uncooked angel hair pasta
- 8 oz. fresh sugar snap peas (about 2 cups), halved diagonally
- 2 Tbsp. olive oil
- 1 lb. uncooked shrimp (26-30 per lb.), peeled and deveined
- 3 tsp. curry powder
- 1 tsp. ground cumin
- ¾ tsp. salt
- 6 green onions, diagonally sliced

1. Cook pasta according to the package directions, adding snap peas during the last 1-2 minutes of cooking. Drain, reserving ½ cup pasta water.

2. In a skillet, heat oil over medium-high heat; saute shrimp 2 minutes. Add seasonings and green onions; cook and stir until the shrimp turn pink, 1-2 minutes. Add pasta and peas; heat through, tossing to combine and adding reserved pasta water if desired.

1⅓ CUPS: 404 cal., 10g fat (1g sat. fat), 138mg chol., 588mg sod., 50g carb. (4g sugars, 5g fiber), 28g pro. **DIABETIC EXCHANGES:** 3 starch, 3 lean meat, 1½ fat.

PEAR PORK CHOPS

You will be tempted to eat this main dish straight out of the pan. But save some for your guests! It's sure to wow them at the dinner table.
—*Taste of Home Test Kitchen*

TAKES: 30 min. • **MAKES:** 4 servings

- 1 pkg. (6 oz.) cornbread stuffing mix
- 4 boneless pork loin chops (6 oz. each)
- ½ tsp. pepper
- ¼ tsp. salt
- 2 Tbsp. butter
- 2 medium pears, chopped
- 1 medium sweet red pepper, chopped
- 2 green onions, thinly sliced

1. Prepare stuffing mix according to package directions. Meanwhile, sprinkle chops with pepper and salt. In a large skillet, brown pork chops in butter. Sprinkle with chopped pears and red pepper.

2. Top with stuffing and onions. Cook, uncovered, over medium heat until a thermometer inserted in pork reads 145°, 8-10 minutes.

1 PORK CHOP WITH ¾ CUP STUFFING MIXTURE: 603 cal., 28g fat (14g sat. fat), 127mg chol., 1094mg sod., 47g carb. (14g sugars, 5g fiber), 38g pro.

CURRIED SHRIMP PASTA

THOMAS FAGLON
Somerset, NJ

PORK MEDALLIONS WITH BRANDY CREAM SAUCE

I adapted this elegant main dish from a recipe my mother-in-law cooked for our family. Cayenne lends a bit of heat to its rich, creamy sauce.
—*Judy Armstrong, Prairieville, LA*

- -

PREP: 25 min. • **COOK:** 25 min.
MAKES: 4 servings

- 12 oz. uncooked linguine
- 1 lb. pork tenderloin, cut into 1-in. slices
- ¼ cup all-purpose flour
- 2 Tbsp. olive oil
- 3 Tbsp. butter, divided
- 1¾ cups sliced baby portobello mushrooms
- 5 green onions, thinly sliced
- 2 garlic cloves, minced
- 1½ cups heavy whipping cream
- ¼ cup brandy
- 2 Tbsp. minced fresh thyme
- 1 Tbsp. Dijon mustard
- ½ tsp. salt
- ½ tsp. pepper
- ¼ tsp. cayenne pepper
- 2 plum tomatoes, seeded and chopped
- 2 Tbsp. shredded Parmesan cheese

1. Cook linguine according to the package directions. Meanwhile, flatten pork slices to ¼-in. thickness. Place flour in a large shallow dish. Add pork, a few pieces at a time, and turn to coat.
2. In a large skillet over medium-high heat, cook pork in oil and 2 Tbsp. butter in batches until the juices run clear, 3-4 minutes on each side. Set aside and keep warm.
3. In the same skillet, saute mushrooms and onions in remaining butter until tender. Add garlic; cook 1 minute longer. Add the cream, brandy, thyme, mustard, salt, pepper and cayenne. Bring to a boil; cook until liquid is reduced by half, about 8 minutes.
4. Drain linguine. Stir tomatoes into sauce mixture; add pork and heat through. Serve with linguine and sprinkle with cheese.
1 SERVING: 937 cal., 55g fat (29g sat. fat), 210mg chol., 577mg sod., 72g carb. (5g sugars, 4g fiber), 39g pro.

ZESTY GRILLED HAM

FAST FIX | 5 INGREDIENTS
ZESTY GRILLED HAM

If it's ham, my kids will eat it, and they like this kicked-up recipe best of all. Even the small ones eat adult-sized portions, so be sure to make plenty.
—*Mary Ann Lien, Tyler, TX*

- -

TAKES: 15 min. • **MAKES:** 4 servings

- ⅓ cup packed brown sugar
- 2 Tbsp. prepared horseradish
- 4 tsp. lemon juice
- 1 fully cooked bone-in ham steak (1 lb.)

1. Place the brown sugar, horseradish and lemon juice in a small saucepan; bring to a boil, stirring constantly. Brush over both sides of ham steak.
2. Place the ham on an oiled grill rack over medium heat. Grill, covered, until ham is glazed and heated through, 7-10 minutes, turning occasionally.
1 SERVING: 180 cal., 5g fat (2g sat. fat), 44mg chol., 845mg sod., 20g carb. (19g sugars, 0 fiber), 14g pro.

SKILLET
MAC & CHEESE

SMART SIDE DISHES

No need to settle for plain veggies to keep your costs down when a tasty and inventive side dish can make any meal feel like a special occasion. Quick, convenient and budget-friendly, these delicious sides are the perfect partner to any entree.

SKILLET MAC & CHEESE

This dish is so simple it seems almost too easy! You'll love it and want to fix it often. Kids really go for the rich cheesy flavor. You can add salt and pepper to taste, but we don't feel it needs it.

—Ann Bowers, Rockport, TX

TAKES: 25 min. • **MAKES:** 4 servings

- 2 cups uncooked elbow macaroni (about 8 oz.)
- 2 Tbsp. butter
- 2 Tbsp. all-purpose flour
- 1½ cups half-and-half cream
- ¾ lb. process cheese (Velveeta), cubed
  Optional toppings: fresh arugula, halved cherry tomatoes and coarsely ground pepper

1. Cook macaroni according to the package directions; drain.

2. Meanwhile, in a large nonstick skillet, melt butter over medium heat. Stir in flour until smooth; gradually whisk in cream. Bring to a boil, stirring constantly. Cook and stir until thickened, about 2 minutes. Reduce heat; stir in cheese until melted.

3. Add the macaroni; cook and stir until heated through. Top as desired.

1½ CUPS: 600 cal., 37g fat (23g sat. fat), 144mg chol., 1185mg sod., 40g carb. (9g sugars, 1g fiber), 23g pro.

MY TWO CENT$

"I have tried many mac and cheese recipes, and this was the best and creamiest so far. It was so easy and quick. And it reheats much better than other mac and cheese recipes I've tried, probably due to the Velveeta. I topped it with fresh parsley and crumbled bacon. This will be my new go-to mac and cheese recipe!"

—NICOLE, TASTEOFHOME.COM

SEASONED FRIES

SEASONED FRIES

Instead of making french fries from scratch, I reach for frozen potatoes and make them my own with Parmesan cheese and Italian seasoning. These are always very popular with my family.

—Maribeth Edwards, Follansbee, WV

TAKES: 15 min. • **MAKES:** 6 servings

- 6 cups frozen shoestring potatoes
- ½ cup grated Parmesan cheese
- 2 tsp. Italian seasoning
- ½ tsp. salt

Place potatoes on a foil-lined baking sheet. Bake at 450° for 8 minutes. Combine the remaining ingredients; sprinkle over the potatoes and mix gently. Bake until potatoes are browned and crisp, 4-5 minutes longer.

¾ CUP: 108 cal., 2g fat (1g sat. fat), 6mg chol., 344mg sod., 18g carb. (1g sugars, 3g fiber), 3g pro.

ZUCCHINI MUSHROOM BAKE

Just a 10-minute prep dresses up zucchini with mushrooms, onion, cheddar and basil.

—Jacquelyn Smith, Carmel, ME

PREP: 10 min. • **BAKE:** 30 min.
MAKES: 4 servings

- 3 cups sliced zucchini
- 2 cups sliced fresh mushrooms
- ⅓ cup sliced onion
- ½ tsp. dried basil
- ¼ tsp. salt
- ½ cup shredded cheddar cheese

1. Preheat oven to 350°. Toss together first five ingredients; place in a greased 2-qt. shallow baking dish.

2. Bake, covered, for 30 minutes. Sprinkle with cheese; bake, uncovered, until the vegetables are tender, about 10 minutes.

⅔ CUP: 83 cal., 5g fat (3g sat. fat), 14mg chol., 249mg sod., 5g carb. (3g sugars, 1g fiber), 5g pro. **DIABETIC EXCHANGES:** 1 medium-fat meat, 1 vegetable.

NO-FUSS
ROLLS

NO-FUSS ROLLS

These four-ingredient rolls are ready in no time. And they are fantastic with herb butter or jam.
—*Glenda Trail, Manchester, TN*

TAKES: 25 min. • **MAKES:** 6 rolls

- 1 cup self-rising flour
- ½ cup 2% milk
- 2 Tbsp. mayonnaise
- ½ tsp. sugar

Preheat oven to 450°. In a small bowl, combine all the ingredients. Spoon into six muffin cups coated with cooking spray. Bake until a toothpick comes out clean, 12-14 minutes. Cool for 5 minutes, then remove from pan to a wire rack. Serve warm.

NOTE: As a substitute for 1 cup of self-rising flour, place 1½ tsp. baking powder and ½ tsp. salt in a measuring cup. Add all-purpose flour to measure 1 cup.

1 SERVING: 111 cal., 4g fat (1g sat. fat), 3mg chol., 275mg sod., 16g carb. (1g sugars, 0 fiber), 3g pro. **DIABETIC EXCHANGES:** 1 starch, 1 fat.

SAUTEED APPLES

Here's a sweet side dish my family loves. It's wonderful with pork or chicken, but you can use it to top pancakes or French toast for breakfast, too.
—*Shirley Heston, Pickerington, OH*

TAKES: 30 min. • **MAKES:** 6 servings

- ¼ cup butter, cubed
- 5 medium Golden Delicious apples, peeled and thinly sliced
- ¼ cup water
- ½ cup sugar
- ½ tsp. ground cinnamon

In a large skillet, heat butter over medium-high heat; saute apples 1 minute. Add water; bring to a boil. Stir in sugar and cinnamon. Reduce heat; simmer, covered, until the apples are tender, 10-12 minutes, stirring occasionally.

⅔ CUP: 185 cal., 8g fat (5g sat. fat), 20mg chol., 61mg sod., 31g carb. (28g sugars, 2g fiber), 0 pro.

HERBED PORTOBELLO PASTA

HERBED PORTOBELLO PASTA

Meaty mushrooms make this light pasta taste hearty and filling. It's my fast and fresh go-to weeknight side dish.
—*Laurie Trombley, Stonyford, CA*

PREP: 20 min. • **COOK:** 15 min.
MAKES: 4 servings

- ½ lb. uncooked multigrain angel hair pasta
- 4 large portobello mushrooms (¾ lb.), stems removed
- 1 Tbsp. olive oil
- 2 garlic cloves, minced
- 4 plum tomatoes, chopped
- ¼ cup pitted Greek olives
- ¼ cup minced fresh basil
- 1 tsp. minced fresh rosemary or ¼ tsp. dried rosemary, crushed
- 1 tsp. minced fresh thyme or ¼ tsp. dried thyme
- ¼ tsp. salt
- ⅛ tsp. pepper
- ⅔ cup crumbled feta cheese
- ¼ cup shredded Parmesan cheese

1. Cook pasta according to the package directions for al dente. Meanwhile, cut mushrooms in half and thinly slice. In a large skillet, heat oil over medium heat. Add the mushrooms; saute until tender, 8-10 minutes. Add garlic; cook for 1 minute longer. Stir in tomatoes and olives. Reduce heat to low; cook, uncovered, until slightly thickened, about 5 minutes. Stir in herbs, salt and pepper.

2. Drain the pasta, reserving ¼ cup of the pasta water. Toss pasta with the mushroom mixture, adjusting consistency with reserved pasta water. Sprinkle with cheeses.

1½ CUPS: 375 cal., 12g fat (4g sat. fat), 14mg chol., 585mg sod., 48g carb. (5g sugars, 7g fiber), 18g pro. **DIABETIC EXCHANGES:** 3 starch, 2 medium-fat meat, 2 fat, 1 vegetable.

OUR TWO CENT$

- This isn't a saucy pasta, so leftovers make a great cold pasta salad for the next day's lunch.

- Instead of adding salt, zest a little lemon over the pasta and squeeze a bit of juice over each serving. It brightens up the flavor and helps keep it healthy.

- If you're not a feta fan, other cheeses are delicious on this dish; try crumbled blue cheese or goat cheese, or even skip the cheese altogether.

CHERRY TOMATO MOZZARELLA SAUTE

This quick side dish is full of flavor. The mix of cherry tomatoes and mozzarella pairs well with almost any main dish.
—*Summer Jones, Pleasant Grove, UT*

TAKES: 25 min. • **MAKES:** 4 servings

- 2   tsp. olive oil
- ¼   cup chopped shallots
- 1   tsp. minced fresh thyme
- 1   garlic clove, minced
- 2½ cups cherry tomatoes, halved
- ¼   tsp. salt
- ¼   tsp. pepper
- 4   oz. fresh mozzarella cheese cut into ½-in. cubes

In a large skillet, heat oil over medium-high heat; saute shallots with thyme until tender. Add garlic; cook and stir 1 minute. Stir in tomatoes, salt and pepper; heat through. Remove from heat; stir in cheese.

⅔ CUP: 127 cal., 9g fat (4g sat. fat), 22mg chol., 194mg sod., 6g carb. (4g sugars, 2g fiber), 6g pro.

PARMESAN ROASTED BROCCOLI

HOLLY SANDER
Lake Mary, FL

PARMESAN ROASTED BROCCOLI

Sure, it's simple and healthy—but, oh, is this roasted broccoli delicious. Cutting the stalks into tall trees turns this ordinary veggie into a standout side dish.
—*Holly Sander, Lake Mary, FL*

TAKES: 30 min. • **MAKES:** 4 servings

- 2   small broccoli crowns (about 8 oz. each)
- 3   Tbsp. olive oil
- ½   tsp. salt
- ½   tsp. pepper
- ¼   tsp. crushed red pepper flakes
- 4   garlic cloves, thinly sliced
- 2   Tbsp. grated Parmesan cheese
- 1   tsp. grated lemon zest

1. Preheat oven to 425°. Cut broccoli crowns into quarters from top to bottom. Drizzle broccoli with oil; sprinkle with salt, pepper and pepper flakes. Place in a parchment paper-lined 15x10x1-in. baking pan.
2. Roast until crisp-tender, 10-12 minutes. Sprinkle with the garlic; roast 5 minutes longer. Sprinkle with cheese; roast until the cheese is melted and the broccoli is tender, 2-4 minutes more. Sprinkle with lemon zest.
2 BROCCOLI PIECES: 144 cal., 11g fat (2g sat. fat), 2mg chol., 378mg sod., 9g carb. (2g sugars, 3g fiber), 4g pro. **DIABETIC EXCHANGES:** 2 fat, 1 vegetable.

LORA'S RED BEANS & RICE

My dear mother-in-law passed this simple recipe to me. With meats, beans and savory veggies that simmer all day, it's tasty, easy and economical, too!
—*Carol Simms, Madison, MS*

- -

PREP: 15 min. + soaking • **COOK:** 8 hours
MAKES: 10 servings

- 1 pkg. (16 oz.) dried kidney beans (about 2½ cups)
- 2 cups cubed fully cooked ham (about 1 lb.)
- 1 pkg. (12 oz.) fully cooked andouille chicken sausage links or flavor of choice, sliced
- 1 medium green pepper, chopped
- 1 medium onion, chopped
- 2 celery ribs, chopped
- 1 Tbsp. hot pepper sauce
- 2 garlic cloves, minced
- 1½ tsp. salt
    Hot cooked rice

1. Place beans in a large bowl; add cool water to cover. Soak overnight.
2. Drain beans, discarding water; rinse with cool water. Place beans in a greased 6-qt. slow cooker. Stir in ham, sausage, vegetables, pepper sauce, garlic and salt. Add water to cover by 1 in.
3. Cook, covered, on low, until beans are tender, 8-9 hours. Serve with rice.

1 CUP BEAN MIXTURE: 249 cal., 5g fat (1g sat. fat), 43mg chol., 906mg sod., 31g carb. (2g sugars, 7g fiber), 23g pro.

LORA'S
RED BEANS
& RICE

SHIITAKE & BUTTERNUT RISOTTO

I like to think of this recipe as a labor of love. The risotto takes a bit of extra attention, but once you take your first bite you'll know it was worth the effort.
—*Stephanie Campbell, Elk Grove, CA*

- -

PREP: 25 min. • **COOK:** 25 min.
MAKES: 2 servings

- 1 cup cubed peeled butternut squash
- 2 tsp. olive oil, divided
    Dash salt
- 1¼ cups reduced-sodium chicken broth
- ⅔ cup sliced fresh shiitake mushrooms
- 2 Tbsp. chopped onion
- 1 small garlic clove, minced
- ⅓ cup uncooked arborio rice
    Dash pepper
- ¼ cup white wine or ¼ cup additional reduced-sodium chicken broth
- ¼ cup grated Parmesan cheese
- 1 tsp. minced fresh sage

1. Preheat oven to 350°. Place squash in a greased 9-in. square baking pan. Add 1 tsp. oil and salt; toss to coat. Bake the squash, uncovered, until tender, 25-30 minutes, stirring occasionally.
2. Meanwhile, in a small saucepan, heat broth and keep warm. In a small skillet, saute the mushrooms, onion and garlic in the remaining oil until tender, 3-4 minutes. Add the rice and pepper; cook and stir for 2-3 minutes. Reduce heat; stir in wine. Cook and stir until all of the liquid is absorbed.
3. Add the heated broth, ¼ cup at a time, stirring constantly. Allow the liquid to absorb between additions. Cook just until risotto is creamy and the rice is almost tender, about 20 minutes. Stir in cheese until melted. Add squash and sage. Serve immediately.

¾ CUP: 282 cal., 9g fat (3g sat. fat), 12mg chol., 567mg sod., 40g carb. (3g sugars, 3g fiber), 10g pro.

OUR TWO CENT$

- Earthy cremini mushrooms make a good substitute for shiitakes.
- If you add the cheese too early, the heat can cause it to break (when fat separates out of a sauce), leading to a greasy, granular dish.

1. In a large bowl, dissolve the yeast in warm water. Stir in the remaining ingredients to form a wet dough; transfer to a greased 2½-qt. baking dish. Cover; let stand in a warm place 1 hour.

2. Stir down dough. Cover; let stand 1 hour. Preheat oven to 425°.

3. Bake 20 minutes. Reduce oven setting to 350°. Bake until top is golden brown and a thermometer inserted in bread reads 210°, about 20 minutes longer.

4. Remove from baking dish to a wire rack to cool. Serve warm.

1 SLICE: 133 cal., 3g fat (0 sat. fat), 0 chol., 296mg sod., 24g carb. (2g sugars, 1g fiber), 3g pro. **DIABETIC EXCHANGES:** 1½ starch, ½ fat.

HEALTH TIP: Some packaged breads have more than 20 ingredients! This loaf includes just six easy-to-pronounce ones.

FAST FIX

VEGETABLE & BARLEY PILAF

This delicious dish is hearty, colorful, easy and fast—that it's good for you is a bonus! Barley has a healthy amount of soluble fiber, which aids digestion, and it can help to lower cholesterol. You can easily substitute other fresh veggies you have on hand.
—*Jesse Klausmeier, Burbank, CA*

- -

TAKES: 30 min. • **MAKES:** 4 servings

- 1   large zucchini, quartered and sliced
- 1   large carrot, chopped
- 1   Tbsp. butter
- 2   cups reduced-sodium chicken broth
- 1   cup quick-cooking barley
- 2   green onions, chopped
- ½   tsp. dried marjoram
- ¼   tsp. salt
- ⅛   tsp. pepper

1. In a large saucepan, saute zucchini and carrot in butter until crisp-tender. Add the broth; bring to a boil. Stir in barley. Reduce heat; cover and simmer until the barley is tender, 10-12 minutes.

2. Stir in the onions, marjoram, salt and pepper. Remove from the heat; cover and let stand for 5 minutes.

SPINACH BARLEY PILAF: Stir in 1 cup chopped fresh spinach when you add the onions.

¾ CUP: 219 cal., 4g fat (2g sat. fat), 8mg chol., 480mg sod., 39g carb. (3g sugars, 10g fiber), 9g pro.

RED WINE CRANBERRY SAUCE

5 INGREDIENTS

RED WINE CRANBERRY SAUCE

While doing some holiday cooking one year, I added half a cup of wine to the cranberry sauce in place of juice. And just like that a new recipe was born!
—*Helen Nelander, Boulder Creek, CA*

- -

PREP: 5 min. • **COOK:** 20 min. + chilling
MAKES: about 2⅓ cups

- 1   pkg. (12 oz.) fresh or frozen cranberries
- 1   cup sugar
- 1   cup water
- ½   cup dry red wine or grape juice

1. In a large saucepan, combine all the ingredients; bring to a boil, stirring to dissolve sugar. Reduce heat to medium; cook, uncovered, until most of the berries pop, about 15 minutes, stirring occasionally.

2. Transfer mixture to a bowl; cool slightly. Refrigerate, covered, until cold (sauce will thicken upon cooling).

¼ CUP: 122 cal., 0 fat (0 sat. fat), 0 chol., 1mg sod., 30g carb. (27g sugars, 2g fiber), 0 pro.

5 INGREDIENTS

ONE-DISH NO-KNEAD BREAD

Don't worry if you're new to baking—anyone who can stir can make this bread!
—*Heather Chambers, Largo, FL*

- -

PREP: 15 min. + rising • **BAKE:** 40 min.
MAKES: 1 loaf (12 slices)

- 1   tsp. active dry yeast
- 1½ cups warm water (110° to 115°)
- 2¾ cups all-purpose flour
- 2   Tbsp. sugar
- 2   Tbsp. olive oil
- 1½ tsp. salt

VEGETABLE &
BARLEY PILAF

ORANGE CORN MUFFINS

This is my revamp of an old recipe—the original had a topping that made these muffins too sweet. Now they're perfect to accompany a meal. Sometimes I make lemon corn muffins by using lemon zest if I don't have an orange on hand. You can add nuts if you'd like; the original recipe called for pecans.

—Hope Huggins, Santa Cruz, CA

- -

PREP: 20 min. • **BAKE:** 15 min.
MAKES: 1 dozen

- 1 cup yellow cornmeal
- 1 cup all-purpose flour
- ⅓ cup sugar
- 4 tsp. baking powder
- ¼ tsp. salt
- 1 large egg, beaten
- 1 cup 2% milk
- ¼ cup canola oil
- 1 Tbsp. grated orange zest

1. Preheat oven to 425°. In a bowl, combine the cornmeal, flour, sugar, baking powder and salt. In another bowl, combine egg, milk, oil and orange zest. Stir into the cornmeal mixture just until moistened.

2. Fill greased muffin cups two-thirds full. Bake until lightly browned, about 15 minutes. Cool for 5 minutes before removing to wire racks. Serve warm.

1 MUFFIN: 161 cal., 6g fat (1g sat. fat), 20mg chol., 198mg sod., 24g carb. (7g sugars, 1g fiber), 3g pro.

FAST FIX | 5 INGREDIENTS

DILLED NEW POTATOES

With six kids at home, I try to grow as much of our own food as possible, and our big potato patch means easy and affordable meals for much of the year. For this fresh and tasty side dish, I season red potatoes with homegrown dill.

—Jennifer Ferris, Bronson, MI

- -

TAKES: 25 min. • **MAKES:** 8 servings

- 2 lbs. baby red potatoes (about 24)
- ¼ cup butter, melted
- 2 Tbsp. snipped fresh dill
- 1 Tbsp. lemon juice
- 1 tsp. salt
- ½ tsp. pepper

1. Place potatoes in a Dutch oven; add water to cover. Bring to a boil. Reduce heat; cook, uncovered, until tender, 15-20 minutes.

2. Drain; return to pan. Mix remaining ingredients; drizzle over potatoes and toss to coat.

¾ CUP: 180 cal., 8g fat (5g sat. fat), 20mg chol., 447mg sod., 27g carb. (1g sugars, 2g fiber), 3g pro. **DIABETIC EXCHANGES:** 2 starch, 1½ fat.

ORANGE CORN MUFFINS

CREAMY LEMON RICE

SALAMI & PROVOLONE PASTA SALAD

This quick and easy pasta salad has all the flavors of your favorite Italian sub! It's terrific when you want something that's fast, light and cool.
—*Jill Donley, Warsaw, IN*

- -

PREP: 25 min. + chilling • **MAKES:** 8 servings

- 3 cups uncooked cellentani pasta or elbow macaroni
- 1 medium sweet red pepper, chopped
- 4 oz. provolone cheese, cubed (about 1 cup)
- 4 oz. hard salami, cubed (about 1 cup)
- ⅓ cup prepared Italian salad dressing
  Additional Italian salad dressing and minced fresh basil, optional

1. Cook pasta according to package directions. Meanwhile, in a large bowl, combine pepper, cheese and salami.
2. Drain the pasta and rinse in cold water. Add to pepper mixture. Drizzle with ⅓ cup dressing and toss to coat. Refrigerate, covered, at least 1 hour. If desired, stir in additional dressing to moisten and sprinkle with basil before serving.
¾ CUP: 244 cal., 12g fat (5g sat. fat), 24mg chol., 575mg sod., 23g carb. (2g sugars, 1g fiber), 11g pro.

FAST FIX
CREAMY LEMON RICE

This lively rice dish has a creamy texture that's reminiscent of a lemon risotto, but without all the fuss. Keep this one in your back pocket for hosting dinner guests— or as a great side any old day!
—*Lyndsay Wells, Ladysmith, BC*

- -

TAKES: 30 min. • **MAKES:** 4 servings

- 2½ cups chicken broth
- 2 oz. cream cheese, cubed
- ½ tsp. grated lemon zest
- 1 Tbsp. lemon juice
- ¼ tsp. salt
- ¼ tsp. coarsely ground pepper
- 1 cup uncooked long grain rice
- ¼ cup minced fresh basil

1. In a saucepan, combine the first six ingredients; bring to a boil. Stir with a whisk to blend.
2. Stir in rice; return to a boil. Reduce heat; simmer, covered, until liquid is absorbed and rice is tender, about 15 minutes. Stir in basil.
¾ CUP: 246 cal., 6g fat (3g sat. fat), 17mg chol., 806mg sod., 42g carb. (1g sugars, 1g fiber), 5g pro.

FAST FIX | 5 INGREDIENTS
EASY HOMEMADE CHUNKY APPLESAUCE

Here's a comforting, homestyle treat that never loses its appeal. Dish up big bowlfuls and wait for the smiles!
—*Marilee Cardinal, Burlington, NJ*

- -

TAKES: 30 min. • **MAKES:** 5 cups

- 7 medium McIntosh, Empire or other apples (about 3 lbs.)
- ½ cup sugar
- ½ cup water
- 1 Tbsp. lemon juice
- ¼ tsp. almond or vanilla extract

1. Peel, core and cut each apple into eight wedges. Cut each wedge crosswise in half; place in a large saucepan. Add remaining ingredients.
2. Bring to a boil. Reduce heat; simmer, covered, until the desired consistency is reached, 15-20 minutes, stirring occasionally.
¾ CUP: 139 cal., 0 fat (0 sat. fat), 0 chol., 0 sod., 36g carb. (33g sugars, 2g fiber), 0 pro.

BLACKENED PORK
CAESAR SALAD

PENNY HEDGES
Dewdney, BC

SOUPS, SALADS & SAMMIES

You can't go wrong with this classic combination. Whether you create an entire menu of sandwiches, greens and soups, or you simply enjoy one of the following recipes, you'll turn to this chapter time again. Easy, quick and economical, these specialties are proven lifesavers for today's home cooks.

BLACKENED PORK CAESAR SALAD

When I cook, the goal is to have enough for lunch the next day. This Caesar salad with pork has fantastic flavor even when the leftover meat has chilled overnight.
—*Penny Hedges, Dewdney, BC*

TAKES: 30 min. • **MAKES:** 2 servings

- 2 Tbsp. mayonnaise
- 1 Tbsp. olive oil
- 1 Tbsp. lemon juice
- 1 garlic clove, minced
- ⅛ tsp. seasoned salt
- ⅛ tsp. pepper

SALAD
- ¾ lb. pork tenderloin, cut into 1-in. cubes
- 1 Tbsp. blackened seasoning
- 1 Tbsp. canola oil
- 6 cups torn romaine
  Shredded Parmesan cheese and salad croutons, optional

1. For dressing, in a small bowl, mix the first six ingredients until blended.
2. Toss pork with blackened seasoning. In a large skillet, heat oil over medium-high heat. Add the pork; cook and stir 5-7 minutes or until tender.
3. To serve, place romaine in a large bowl; add dressing and toss to coat. Top with pork, and, if desired, croutons and cheese.
2½ CUPS: 458 cal., 31g fat (5g sat. fat), 100mg chol., 464mg sod., 8g carb. (2g sugars, 3g fiber), 36g pro.

MY TWO CENT$

"Simple and tasty. I never thought of adding pork to a Caesar salad. The dressing was refreshing and light, but to save even more time your favorite prepared Caesar dressing would work just as well."

—JUSTMBETH, TASTEOFHOME.COM

BASIL BLTS

BASIL BLTS

Everybody goes for the bacon in this impressive sandwich, but it's the lemon spread that makes it special. I love it with garden-fresh tomatoes and basil.
—*Alisa Lewis, Veradale, WA*

TAKES: 15 min. • **MAKES:** 4 servings

- ¼ cup mayonnaise
- 2 Tbsp. minced fresh basil
- 1 tsp. lemon juice
- ¼ tsp. salt
- ⅛ tsp. garlic powder
- 8 thick slices French bread (diagonally cut), toasted
- 4 lettuce leaves
- 2 medium tomatoes, each cut into four slices
- 8 cooked bacon strips

In a small bowl, mix the first five ingredients. Spread over four slices of bread; top with the lettuce, tomatoes, bacon and remaining slices of bread.
1 SANDWICH: 319 cal., 20g fat (5g sat. fat), 28mg chol., 833mg sod., 22g carb. (2g sugars, 2g fiber), 12g pro.
HEALTH TIP: Cut 100 calories and 10 grams of fat by switching from mayonnaise to nonfat Greek yogurt.

LEMONY ZUCCHINI RIBBONS

Fresh zucchini gets a shave and a drizzle of citrus goodness in this fab salad. Sprinkle on the goat cheese or feta and dive in.
—*Ellie Martin Cliffe, Milwaukee, WI*

TAKES: 15 min. • **MAKES:** 4 servings

- 1 Tbsp. olive oil
- ½ tsp. grated lemon zest
- 1 Tbsp. lemon juice
- ½ tsp. salt
- ¼ tsp. pepper
- 3 medium zucchini
- ⅓ cup crumbled goat or feta cheese

1. For dressing, in a small bowl, mix first five ingredients. Using a vegetable peeler, shave the zucchini lengthwise into very thin slices; arrange on a serving plate.
2. To serve, drizzle with dressing and toss lightly to coat. Top with cheese.
¾ CUP: 83 cal., 6g fat (2g sat. fat), 12mg chol., 352mg sod., 5g carb. (3g sugars, 2g fiber), 3g pro. **DIABETIC EXCHANGES:** 1 vegetable, 1 fat.
HEALTH TIP: By making this colorful salad with zucchini instead of spaghetti, you save 130 calories per serving.

PEA SOUP
WITH QUINOA

PEA SOUP WITH QUINOA

This soup is low in fat and high in fiber. Best of all, it has a fantastically fresh flavor and wonderful texture. It doesn't cost much to prepare and it's so simple to make.
—*Jane Hacker, Milwaukee, WI*

- -

PREP: 10 min. • **COOK:** 25 min.
MAKES: 6 servings

- 1 cup water
- ½ cup quinoa, rinsed
- 2 tsp. canola oil
- 1 medium onion, chopped
- 2½ cups frozen peas (about 10 oz.)
- 2 cans (14½ oz. each) reduced-sodium chicken broth or vegetable broth
- ½ tsp. salt
- ¼ tsp. pepper
  Optional toppings: plain yogurt, croutons, shaved Parmesan cheese and cracked pepper

1. In a small saucepan, bring water to a boil. Add quinoa. Reduce heat; simmer, covered, until water is absorbed, 12-15 minutes.
2. Meanwhile, in a large saucepan, heat oil over medium-high heat; saute onion until tender. Stir in peas and broth; bring to a boil. Reduce heat; simmer, uncovered, until peas are tender, about 5 minutes.
3. Puree soup using an immersion blender, or cool slightly and puree soup in a blender; return to pan. Stir in the quinoa, salt and pepper; heat through. Serve with toppings as desired.
1 CUP: 126 cal., 3g fat (0 sat. fat), 0 chol., 504mg sod., 19g carb. (4g sugars, 4g fiber), 7g pro.

MY TWO CENT$

"I have made this recipe many times, and we enjoy it so much. It has excellent flavor and is so good for you. When I cook the quinoa I add chicken stock."
—YAJOHNSON, TASTEOFHOME.COM

HUMMUS
& VEGGIE
WRAP-UP

HUMMUS & VEGGIE WRAP-UP

I had a sandwich similar to this once when I stopped at a diner during a long walk. I enjoyed it so much that I modified it to my liking and now have it for lunch regularly.
—*Michael Steffens, Indianapolis, IN*

- -

TAKES: 15 min. • **MAKES:** 1 serving

- 2 Tbsp. hummus
- 1 whole wheat tortilla (8 in.)
- ¼ cup torn mixed salad greens
- 2 Tbsp. finely chopped sweet onion
- 2 Tbsp. thinly sliced cucumber
- 2 Tbsp. alfalfa sprouts
- 2 Tbsp. shredded carrot
- 1 Tbsp. balsamic vinaigrette

Spread hummus over tortilla. Layer with the salad greens, onion, cucumber, sprouts and carrot. Drizzle with vinaigrette. Roll up tightly. Serve immediately.
1 WRAP: 235 cal., 8g fat (1g sat. fat), 0 chol., 415mg sod., 32g carb. (4g sugars, 5g fiber), 7g pro. **DIABETIC EXCHANGES:** 2 starch, 1 fat.

PINEAPPLE COLESLAW

Pineapple adds pizazz to traditional coleslaw, introducing both color and sweetness. A fast salad, it's sure to be in demand at your next barbecue.
—*Cheryl Dolan, Innerkip, ON*

- -

TAKES: 15 min. • **MAKES:** 4 servings

- 3 cups shredded cabbage
- ¾ cup shredded carrot
- 1 can (8 oz.) unsweetened crushed pineapple, drained
- ⅓ cup mayonnaise
- 4 tsp. sugar
- 4 tsp. white vinegar

In a small bowl, combine the cabbage, carrot and pineapple. In another small bowl, whisk the mayonnaise, sugar and vinegar; pour over the pineapple mixture; toss to coat. Serve immediately.
¾ CUP: 206 cal., 15g fat (2g sat. fat), 7mg chol., 126mg sod., 18g carb. (12g sugars, 2g fiber), 1g pro.

BEAN & BACON GRIDDLE BURRITOS

These griddle burritos with bacon and veggies make an awesome hand-held meal. A jar of salsa works if that's what you've got, but I use fresh pico de gallo when I can.
—*Stacy Mullens, Gresham, OR*

- -

TAKES: 20 min. • **MAKES:** 4 servings

- 1   can (16 oz.) fat-free refried beans
- ½   cup salsa, divided
- 4   flour tortillas (8 in.)
- ½   cup crumbled cotija cheese or shredded Monterey Jack cheese
- 3   bacon strips, cooked and coarsely chopped
- 2   cups shredded lettuce

1. In a small bowl, mix beans and ¼ cup salsa until blended. Place tortillas on a griddle; cook over medium heat 1 minute, then turn over. Place bean mixture, cheese and bacon onto centers of tortillas; cook until tortillas begin to crisp, 1-2 minutes longer.
2. Remove from griddle; immediately top with lettuce and remaining salsa. To serve, fold bottom and sides of tortilla over filling.
1 BURRITO: 375 cal., 10g fat (4g sat. fat), 21mg chol., 1133mg sod., 52g carb. (1g sugars, 8g fiber), 18g pro.
HEALTH TIP: Use low-sodium refried beans to save as much as 300 milligrams of sodium per burrito.

CAROLINA-STYLE
VINEGAR BBQ CHICKEN

CAROLINA-STYLE VINEGAR BBQ CHICKEN

I live in Georgia but I appreciate the tangy, sweet and slightly spicy taste of Carolina vinegar chicken. I make my version in the slow cooker. With the tempting aroma filling the house, your family is sure to be at the dinner table on time!
—*Ramona Parris, Canton, GA*

- -

PREP: 10 min. • **COOK:** 4 hours
MAKES: 6 servings

- 2   cups water
- 1   cup white vinegar
- ¼   cup sugar
- 1   Tbsp. reduced-sodium chicken base
- 1   tsp. crushed red pepper flakes
- ¾   tsp. salt
- 1½   lbs. boneless skinless chicken breasts
- 6   whole wheat hamburger buns, split, optional

1. In a bowl, mix the first six ingredients. Place chicken in a 3-qt. slow cooker; add vinegar mixture. Cook, covered, on low for 4-5 hours or until chicken is tender.
2. Remove the chicken; cool slightly. Reserve 1 cup cooking juices; discard the remaining juices. Shred chicken with two forks. Return meat and the reserved cooking juices to the slow cooker; heat through. If desired, serve chicken mixture on buns.
NOTE: Look for chicken base near the broth and bouillon.
½ CUP: 134 cal., 3g fat (1g sat. fat), 63mg chol., 228mg sod., 3g carb. (3g sugars, 0 fiber), 23g pro. **DIABETIC EXCHANGES:** 3 lean meat.

EASY WHITE CHICKEN CHILI

Chili is one of our favorite ways to beat the cold weather. We use chicken and white beans for a twist on the regular version. It's soothing comfort food.
—*Rachel Lewis, Danville, VA*

TAKES: 30 min. • **MAKES:** 6 servings

- 1   lb. lean ground chicken
- 1   medium onion, chopped
- 2   cans (15 oz. each) cannellini beans, rinsed and drained
- 1   can (4 oz.) chopped green chilies
- 1   tsp. ground cumin
- ½   tsp. dried oregano
- ¼   tsp. pepper
- 1   can (14½ oz.) reduced-sodium chicken broth
     Optional toppings: reduced-fat sour cream, shredded cheddar cheese and chopped fresh cilantro

1. In a large saucepan, cook the chicken and onion over medium-high heat 6-8 minutes or until chicken is no longer pink, breaking up chicken into crumbles.

2. Pour one can of beans in a small bowl; mash slightly. Stir mashed beans, remaining can of beans, chilies, seasonings and broth into the chicken mixture; bring to a boil. Reduce heat; simmer, covered, until the flavors are blended, 12-15 minutes. Serve with toppings as desired.

FREEZE OPTION: Freeze cooled chili in freezer containers. To use, partially thaw in refrigerator overnight. Heat through in a saucepan, stirring occasionally and adding a little broth if necessary.

1 CUP: 228 cal., 5g fat (1g sat. fat), 54mg chol., 504mg sod., 23g carb. (1g sugars, 6g fiber), 22g pro. **DIABETIC EXCHANGES:** 3 lean meat, 1½ starch.

EASY WHITE CHICKEN CHILI

CHICKEN TZATZIKI CUCUMBER BOATS

I've tended a garden for decades, and these colorful boats made from cucumbers hold my fresh tomatoes, peas and dill. The boats are absolute garden greatness.
—*Ronna Farley, Rockville, MD*

TAKES: 15 min. • **MAKES:** 2 servings

- 2   medium cucumbers
- ½   cup fat-free plain Greek yogurt
- 2   Tbsp. mayonnaise
- ½   tsp. garlic salt
- 3   tsp. snipped fresh dill, divided
- 1   cup chopped cooked chicken breast
- 1   cup chopped seeded tomato (about 1 large), divided
- ½   cup fresh or frozen peas, thawed

1. Cut each cucumber lengthwise in half; scoop out pulp, leaving a ¼-in. shell. In a bowl, mix yogurt, mayonnaise, garlic salt and 1 tsp. dill; gently stir in chicken, ¾ cup tomato and peas.

2. Spoon into cucumber shells. Top with the remaining tomato and dill.

2 FILLED CUCUMBER HALVES: 312 cal., 12g fat (2g sat. fat), 55mg chol., 641mg sod., 18g carb. (10g sugars, 6g fiber), 34g pro. **DIABETIC EXCHANGES:** 4 lean meat, 2 vegetable, 2 fat, ½ starch.

HEALTH TIP: Skip the peas for a fast and refreshing low-carb lunch or supper.

SPINACH & SAUSAGE
LENTIL SOUP

SPINACH & SAUSAGE
LENTIL SOUP

During the cooler months of the year, this soup makes regular appearances on our dinner table. It is approved by all, including my picky 6-year-old.
—Kalyn Gensic, Ardmore, OK

PREP: 5 min. • **COOK:** 45 min.
MAKES: 6 servings (2 qt.)

- 1 lb. bulk spicy pork sausage
- 1 cup dried brown lentils, rinsed
- 1 can (15 oz.) cannellini beans, rinsed and drained
- 1 carton (32 oz.) reduced-sodium chicken broth
- 1 cup water
- 1 can (14½ oz.) fire-roasted diced tomatoes, undrained
- 6 cups fresh spinach (about 4 oz.)
   Crumbled goat cheese, optional

1. In a Dutch oven, cook and crumble the sausage over medium heat until no longer pink, 5-7 minutes; drain.
2. Stir in lentils, beans, broth and water; bring to a boil. Reduce heat; simmer, covered, until lentils are tender, about 30 minutes. Stir in tomatoes; heat through.
3. Remove from heat; stir in spinach until wilted. If desired, serve with goat cheese.
FREEZE OPTION: Freeze cooled soup in freezer containers. To use, partially thaw in refrigerator overnight. Heat through in a saucepan, stirring occasionally.
1⅓ CUPS: 390 cal., 17g fat (5g sat. fat), 41mg chol., 1242mg sod., 37g carb. (3g sugars, 8g fiber), 22g pro.

SLOW COOKER

TANGY PULLED PORK SANDWICHES

The slow cooker not only makes this a no-fuss meal, but it keeps the pork tender, moist and loaded with flavor. The sandwiches are so comforting, and the recipe is easy and economical.
—Beki Kosydar-Krantz, Mayfield, PA

PREP: 10 min. • **COOK:** 4 hours
MAKES: 4 servings

- 1 pork tenderloin (1 lb.)
- 1 cup ketchup
- 2 Tbsp. plus 1½ tsp. brown sugar
- 2 Tbsp. plus 1½ tsp. cider vinegar
- 1 Tbsp. plus 1½ tsp. Worcestershire sauce
- 1 Tbsp. spicy brown mustard
- ¼ tsp. pepper
- 4 rolls or buns, split and toasted
   Coleslaw, optional

1. Cut the tenderloin in half; place in a 3-qt. slow cooker. Combine the ketchup, brown sugar, vinegar, Worcestershire sauce, mustard and pepper; pour over pork.
2. Cover and cook on low for 4-5 hours or until meat is tender. Remove meat; shred with two forks. Return to slow cooker; heat through. Serve on toasted rolls or buns, with coleslaw, if desired.
1 SERVING: 402 cal., 7g fat (2g sat. fat), 63mg chol., 1181mg sod., 56g carb. (18g sugars, 2g fiber), 29g pro.

OUR TWO CENT$

Light brown sugar has a delicate flavor while dark brown sugar has a slightly stronger molasses flavor. They can be used interchangeably, so use whatever brown sugar you have on hand for these sandwiches and avoid a trip to the supermarket.

**TANGY PULLED PORK
SANDWICHES**

FAST FIX

CRISPY PORK TENDERLOIN SANDWICHES

This breaded tenderloin rekindles memories of a sandwich shop in my Ohio hometown. Even though I've moved away, I'm happy that my family can still enjoy the sandwich thanks to this quick recipe.
—*Erin Fitch, Sherrills Ford, NC*

TAKES: 25 min. • **MAKES:** 4 servings

- 2 Tbsp. all-purpose flour
- ½ tsp. salt
- ¼ tsp. pepper
- 1 large egg, lightly beaten
- ½ cup seasoned bread crumbs
- 3 Tbsp. panko (Japanese) bread crumbs
- ½ lb. pork tenderloin
- 2 Tbsp. canola oil
- 4 hamburger buns or kaiser rolls, split
  Optional toppings: lettuce leaves, tomato and pickle slices, and mayonnaise

1. In a shallow bowl, mix the flour, salt and pepper. Place egg in another shallow bowl. Combine bread crumbs and place in a third shallow bowl.

2. Cut tenderloin crosswise into four slices; pound each with a meat mallet to ¼-in. thickness. Dip in flour mixture to coat both sides; shake off excess. Dip in egg, then in crumb mixture, patting to help adhere.

3. In a large skillet, heat oil over medium heat. Cook pork 2-3 minutes on each side or until golden brown. Remove from pan; drain on paper towels. Serve in buns, with toppings as desired.

1 SANDWICH: 289 cal., 11g fat (2g sat. fat), 43mg chol., 506mg sod., 29g carb. (3g sugars, 1g fiber), 17g pro. **DIABETIC EXCHANGES:** 2 starch, 2 lean meat, 1½ fat.

HEALTH TIP: Cut carbs to about 10 grams per serving by skipping the bun and serving the pork alone or over grilled portobello mushrooms or sauteed eggplant slices.

FAST FIX

CILANTRO SALAD DRESSING

Use this zippy dressing over greens, as a sandwich spread or even over baked potatoes. You'll love it.
—*Sara Laber, Shelburne, VT*

TAKES: 10 min. • **MAKES:** about ½ cup

- ¼ cup buttermilk
- ¼ cup fat-free mayonnaise
- 3 to 6 drops hot pepper sauce
- ¼ tsp. salt
- ¼ tsp. garlic powder
- ⅛ tsp. sugar
- ½ cup fresh cilantro leaves

Place all ingredients in a blender; cover and process until blended. Refrigerate, covered, until serving.

2 TBSP.: 18 cal., 0 fat (0 sat. fat), 1mg chol., 298mg sod., 4g carb. (2g sugars, 0 fiber), 1g pro.

CRISPY PORK TENDERLOIN SANDWICHES

SUE GRONHOLZ
Beaver Dam, WI

BASIL & HEIRLOOM
TOMATO TOSS

SHORTCUT SAUSAGE MINESTRONE

I call this surprisingly good dish my "magic soup" because of its soothing powers. My daughter-in-law always asks for it when she needs a healing touch.

—*Marta Smith, Claremont, PA*

- -

TAKES: 25 min. • **MAKES:** 6 servings (2 qt.)

¾	lb. Italian turkey sausage links, casings removed
1	small green pepper, chopped
1	small onion, chopped
2	cups cut fresh green beans or frozen cut green beans
2	cups water
1	can (16 oz.) kidney beans, rinsed and drained
1	can (14½ oz.) diced tomatoes with basil, oregano and garlic, undrained
1	can (14½ oz.) reduced-sodium chicken broth
¾	cup uncooked ditalini or other small pasta

1. In a 6-qt. stockpot, cook sausage, pepper and onion over medium heat 5-7 minutes or until sausage is no longer pink, breaking up sausage into crumbles; drain.

2. Add green beans, water, kidney beans, tomatoes and broth; bring to a boil. Stir in ditalini; cook, uncovered, 10-11 minutes or until pasta is tender, stirring occasionally.

1⅓ CUPS: 232 cal., 4g fat (1g sat. fat), 21mg chol., 773mg sod., 34g carb. (6g sugars, 7g fiber), 16g pro.

BASIL & HEIRLOOM TOMATO TOSS

I came up with this garden-fresh salad to showcase the heirloom tomatoes and peppers we grow. Try out other types of basil such as lemon, lime, cinnamon and even licorice.

—*Sue Gronholz, Beaver Dam, WI*

- -

TAKES: 15 min. • **MAKES:** 4 servings

¼	cup olive oil
3	Tbsp. red wine vinegar
2	tsp. sugar
1	garlic clove, minced
¾	tsp. salt
¼	tsp. ground mustard
¼	tsp. pepper
2	large heirloom tomatoes, cut into ½-in. pieces
1	medium sweet yellow pepper, cut into ½-in. pieces
½	small red onion, thinly sliced
1	Tbsp. chopped fresh basil

In a large bowl, whisk the first seven ingredients until blended. Add remaining ingredients; toss gently to combine.

1 CUP: 162 cal., 14g fat (2g sat. fat), 0 chol., 449mg sod., 10g carb. (5g sugars, 2g fiber), 1g pro. **DIABETIC EXCHANGES:** 3 fat, 1 vegetable.

BARBECUE
CHICKEN
TOSTADAS

ECONOMICAL ODDS & ENDS

From oven-fresh breads and pickled classics to hearty sides and appetizers
that double as light entrees, these recipes offer additional ways to save!
Keep money in your wallet when you make your own spaghetti sauce,
apple butter and satisfying snacks folks can't get enough of. You'll find
all of these tantalizing extras and more on the pages that follow.

BARBECUE CHICKEN TOSTADAS

Lots of my recipes start out as economical ways to use leftovers—like this one! My kids love tostadas, so this day-after-cookout dinner was a big hit.

—*Lauren Wyler, Dripping Springs, TX*

TAKES: 30 min. • **MAKES:** 4 servings

- 2 Tbsp. lemon juice
- 2 Tbsp. mayonnaise
- 1 Tbsp. light brown sugar
- ⅛ tsp. pepper
- 2 cups coleslaw mix
- 2 green onions, thinly sliced
- 1 cup baked beans
- 2⅔ cups shredded cooked chicken
- ⅔ cup barbecue sauce
- 8 tostada shells
- 1 cup shredded smoked cheddar cheese

1. Preheat broiler. Mix first four ingredients; toss with coleslaw mix and green onions. Refrigerate until serving.

2. Place beans in a small saucepan; mash with a potato masher until smooth. Cook beans over low heat until heated through, about 10 minutes, stirring frequently.

3. Meanwhile, in another saucepan, mix the chicken and barbecue sauce; cook over medium-low heat until heated through, about 10 minutes, stirring occasionally.

4. To assemble, place the tostada shells on ungreased baking sheets. Spread with beans; top with chicken mixture and cheese. Broil 3-4 in. from heat 1-2 minutes or until tostada shells are lightly browned and the cheese is melted. Top with slaw. Serve immediately.

2 TOSTADAS: 612 cal., 29g fat (10g sat. fat), 116mg chol., 1113mg sod., 51g carb. (21g sugars, 6g fiber), 39g pro.

OUR TWO CENT$

Don't have tostadas on hand? Skip the broiler and simply roll up the heated bean and chicken mixtures in flour tortillas with the dressed coleslaw and cheese.

REFRIGERATOR JALAPENO DILL PICKLES

REFRIGERATOR JALAPENO DILL PICKLES

I'm passionate about making pickles. My husband is passionate about eating them. He's too impatient to let them cure on the shelf, so I found this quick recipe to make him happy. Add hotter peppers if you'd like.

—*Annie Jensen, Roseau, MN*

PREP: 20 min. + chilling
MAKES: about 4 dozen pickle spears

- 3 lbs. pickling cucumbers (about 12)
- 1 small onion, halved and sliced
- ¼ cup snipped fresh dill
- 1 to 2 jalapeno peppers, sliced
- 3 garlic cloves, minced
- 2½ cups water
- 2½ cups cider vinegar
- ⅓ cup canning salt
- ⅓ cup sugar

1. Cut each cucumber lengthwise into four spears. In a very large bowl, combine the cucumbers, onion, dill, jalapenos and garlic. In a large saucepan, combine water, vinegar, salt and sugar. Bring to a boil; cook and stir just until salt and sugar are dissolved. Pour over cucumber mixture; cool.

2. Cover tightly and refrigerate for at least 24 hours. Store in the refrigerator for up to 2 months.

NOTE: Wear disposable gloves when cutting hot peppers; the oils can burn skin. Avoid touching your face.

1 PICKLE: 4 cal., 0 fat (0 sat. fat), 0 chol., 222mg sod., 1g carb. (0 sugars, 0 fiber), 0 pro.

PIZZA ON A STICK

PIZZA ON A STICK

My daughter and her friends had fun turning sausage, pepperoni, veggies and pizza dough into these cute kabobs.
—*Charlene Woods, Norfolk, VA*

- -

TAKES: 30 min. • **MAKES:** 5 servings

8	oz. Italian turkey sausage links
2	cups whole fresh mushrooms
2	cups cherry tomatoes
1	medium onion, cut into 1-in. pieces
1	large green pepper, cut into 1-in. pieces
30	slices turkey pepperoni (2 oz.)
1	tube (13.8 oz.) refrigerated pizza crust
1½	cups shredded part-skim mozzarella cheese
1¼	cups pizza sauce, warmed

1. Preheat oven to 400°. In a large nonstick skillet, cook sausage over medium heat until no longer pink; drain. When cool enough to handle, cut the sausage into 20 pieces. On 10 metal or wooden skewers, alternately thread sausage, vegetables and pepperoni.

2. Unroll pizza dough onto a lightly floured surface; cut widthwise into 1-in.-wide strips. Starting at the pointed end of a prepared skewer, pierce skewer through one end of a dough strip. Spiral-wrap dough strip around skewer, allowing vegetables and meats to peek through. Wrap the remaining end of dough strip around skewer above the first ingredient. Repeat with remaining dough strips and prepared skewers.

3. Arrange kabobs on a baking sheet coated with cooking spray. Bake 10-12 minutes or until vegetables are tender and pizza crust is golden. Immediately sprinkle with cheese. Serve with pizza sauce.

2 KABOBS WITH ¼ CUP SAUCE: 400 cal., 13g fat (5g sat. fat), 58mg chol., 1208mg sod., 42g carb. (0 sugars, 4g fiber), 28g pro. **DIABETIC EXCHANGES:** 3 lean meat, 2 starch, 2 vegetable, 1 fat.

QUINOA UNSTUFFED PEPPERS

QUINOA UNSTUFFED PEPPERS

This fast and easy deconstructed stuffed pepper dish packs a wallop of flavor. Not only do I make it all the time, but I stock my freezer with single-serve portions. They are perfect to take to work and heat up in a microwave for weekday lunches.
—*Rebecca Ende, Phoenix, NY*

- -

TAKES: 30 min. • **MAKES:** 4 servings

1½	cups vegetable stock
¾	cup quinoa, rinsed
1	lb. Italian turkey sausage links, casings removed
1	medium sweet red pepper, chopped
1	medium green pepper, chopped
¾	cup chopped sweet onion
1	garlic clove, minced
¼	tsp. garam masala
¼	tsp. pepper
⅛	tsp. salt

1. In a small saucepan, bring stock to a boil. Add quinoa. Reduce heat; simmer, covered, until the liquid is absorbed, 12-15 minutes. Remove from heat.

2. In a large skillet, cook and crumble sausage with peppers and onion over medium-high heat until no longer pink, 8-10 minutes. Add garlic and seasonings; cook and stir 1 minute. Stir in quinoa.

FREEZE OPTION: Place cooled quinoa mixture in freezer containers. To use, partially thaw in refrigerator overnight. Microwave, covered, on high in a microwave-safe dish until heated through, stirring occasionally.

1 CUP: 261 cal., 9g fat (2g sat. fat), 42mg chol., 760mg sod., 28g carb. (3g sugars, 4g fiber), 17g pro. **DIABETIC EXCHANGES:** 2 starch, 2 medium-fat meat.

OUR TWO CENT$

If you don't keep vegetable stock on hand, chicken or beef stock could also be used. Broth can be used too, but think of stock as a blank canvas where you can layer on the flavors. Broth is already seasoned.

NUTTY APPLE BUTTER

I love apple-picking season. Grab some apples and peanut butter to make this creamy PB&J riff. Spread it on a sandwich or dunk in sliced fruit or graham crackers.
—*Brandie Cranshaw, Rapid City, SD*

- -

PREP: 20 min. • **COOK:** 8 hours
MAKES: 5 cups

- 4 lbs. apples (about 8 large), peeled and chopped
- ¾ to 1 cup sugar
- ¼ cup water
- 3 tsp. ground cinnamon
- ¼ tsp. ground nutmeg
- ¼ tsp. ground cloves
- ¼ tsp. ground allspice
- ¼ cup creamy peanut butter

1. In a greased 5-qt. slow cooker, combine the first seven ingredients. Cook, covered, on low 8-10 hours or until apples are tender.
2. Whisk in peanut butter until apple mixture is smooth. Cool to room temperature. Store in an airtight container in the refrigerator.
2 TBSP.: 43 cal., 1g fat (0 sat. fat), 0 chol., 7mg sod., 9g carb. (8g sugars, 1g fiber), 0 pro.
DIABETIC EXCHANGES: ½ starch.

CYNDY GERKEN
Naples, FL

EVERYTHING BAGEL
CHICKEN STRIPS

FAST FIX
EVERYTHING BAGEL CHICKEN STRIPS

I incorporated the incredible flavor of an everything bagel into a recipe for chicken fingers. Serve these tasty bites with your favorite dipping sauce as an entree, an appetizer or even alongside grilled burgers.
—*Cyndy Gerken, Naples, FL*

- -

TAKES: 30 min. • **MAKES:** 4 servings

- 1 day-old everything bagel, torn
- ½ cup panko (Japanese) bread crumbs
- ½ cup grated Parmesan cheese
- ¼ tsp. crushed red pepper flakes
- ¼ cup butter, cubed
- 1 lb. chicken tenderloins
- ½ tsp. salt

1. Preheat oven to 425°. Pulse torn bagel in a food processor until coarse crumbs form. Place ½ cup bagel crumbs in a shallow bowl; toss with panko bread crumbs, cheese and pepper flakes. (Save remaining bagel crumbs for another use.)

2. In a microwave-safe shallow bowl, microwave butter until melted. Sprinkle chicken with salt. Dip in warm butter, then coat with crumb mixture, patting to help adhere. Place chicken on a greased rack in a 15x10x1-in. baking pan.
3. Bake until golden brown and chicken is no longer pink, 15-17 minutes.
1 SERVING: 246 cal., 12g fat (7g sat. fat), 85mg chol., 593mg sod., 6g carb. (0 sugars, 0 fiber), 30g pro.

OUR TWO CENT$
Baking breaded foods on a rack allows the bottom to crisp up better. If you don't have a rack that will fit in your pan, you can also use a broiler pan with a rack.

POTATO-SAUSAGE FOIL PACKS

We had these smoky campfire bundles at a friend's house and loved the simplicity of this dish. Now we often make the packs for weeknight dinners.
—*Alissa Keith, Forest, VA*

- -

PREP: 20 min. • **GRILL:** 30 min.
MAKES: 4 servings

- 1 medium green pepper
- 1 medium sweet red pepper
- 1 medium sweet yellow pepper
- 1 pkg. (14 oz.) smoked turkey kielbasa, sliced
- 2 large potatoes, cut into wedges
- 1 medium onion, chopped
- 4 tsp. lemon juice
- 4 tsp. olive oil
- ½ tsp. garlic powder
- ½ tsp. pepper
    Lemon wedges, optional

1. Cut peppers into 1-in. pieces; place in a large bowl. Toss the peppers with the next seven ingredients. Divide the mixture among four double thicknesses of heavy-duty foil (about 18x12 in.). Fold foil around mixture, sealing tightly.
2. Grill, covered, over medium heat until potatoes are tender, 30-35 minutes. Open foil carefully to allow steam to escape. If desired, serve with lemon wedges.

1 PACKET: 344 cal., 10g fat (2g sat. fat), 62mg chol., 990mg sod., 42g carb. (8g sugars, 6g fiber), 21g pro.

WALKING TACOS

These popular walking tacos are perfect for everything from a late-night snack to an on-the-go dinner. They're so easy. The ingredients go right into the chip bags!
—*Beverly Matthews, Pasco, WA*

- -

PREP: 10 min. • **COOK:** 30 min.
MAKES: 5 servings

- 1 lb. ground beef
- 1 envelope reduced-sodium chili seasoning mix
- ¼ tsp. pepper
- 1 can (10 oz.) diced tomatoes and green chilies
- 1 can (15 oz.) Ranch Style beans (pinto beans in seasoned tomato sauce)
- 5 pkg. (1 oz. each) corn chips
    Toppings: shredded cheddar cheese, sour cream and sliced green onions

1. In a large skillet, cook beef over medium heat 6-8 minutes or until no longer pink, breaking into crumbles; drain. Stir in the chili seasoning mix, pepper, tomatoes and beans; bring to a boil. Reduce heat; simmer, uncovered, 20-25 minutes or until thickened, stirring occasionally.
2. Just before serving, cut open the corn chip bags. Carefully add the beef mixture and toppings.

1 SERVING: 530 cal., 28g fat (6g sat. fat), 56mg chol., 1017mg sod., 44g carb. (5g sugars, 6g fiber), 24g pro.

POTATO-SAUSAGE
FOIL PACKS

EGGPLANT
FLATBREAD
PIZZAS

CHRISTINE WENDLAND
Browns Mills, NJ

BUFFALO CHICKEN BISCUITS

These spicy, savory muffins are always a hit at parties. We love them as a simple bite on game day, too.
—Jasmin Baron, Livonia, NY

- -

PREP: 20 min. • **BAKE:** 25 min.
MAKES: 1 dozen

    3   cups chopped rotisserie chicken
    ¼   cup Louisiana-style hot sauce
    2   cups biscuit/baking mix
    ¼   tsp. celery seed
    ⅛   tsp. pepper
    1   large egg
    ½   cup 2% milk
    ¼   cup ranch salad dressing
    1½ cups shredded Colby-Monterey
        Jack cheese, divided
    2   green onions, thinly sliced
        Additional ranch dressing and hot
        sauce, optional

1. Preheat oven to 400°. Toss the chicken with hot sauce. In large bowl, whisk together the baking mix, celery seed and pepper. In another bowl, whisk together egg, milk and dressing; add to dry ingredients, stirring just until moistened. Fold in 1 cup cheese, green onions and chicken mixture.
2. Spoon mixture into 12 greased muffin cups. Sprinkle with remaining cheese. Bake until a toothpick inserted in center comes out clean, 25-30 minutes.
3. Cool 5 minutes before removing from pan to a wire rack. Serve warm. If desired, serve with additional dressing and hot sauce. Refrigerate leftovers.
2 MUFFINS: 461 cal., 24g fat (10g sat. fat), 121mg chol., 1180mg sod., 29g carb. (3g sugars, 1g fiber), 31g pro.

FAST FIX
EGGPLANT FLATBREAD PIZZAS

Prepared flatbreads make these tasty pizzas lifesavers on busy weeknights.
—Christine Wendland, Browns Mills, NJ

- -

TAKES: 30 min. • **MAKES:** 4 servings

    3   Tbsp. olive oil, divided
    2½ cups cubed eggplant (½ in.)
    1   small onion, halved and thinly sliced
    ½   tsp. salt
    ⅛   tsp. pepper
    1   garlic clove, minced
    2   naan flatbreads
    ½   cup part-skim ricotta cheese
    1   tsp. dried oregano
    ½   cup roasted garlic tomato sauce
    ½   cup loosely packed basil leaves
    1   cup shredded part-skim
        mozzarella cheese
    2   Tbsp. grated Parmesan cheese
        Sliced fresh basil, optional

1. Preheat oven to 400°. In a large skillet, heat 1 Tbsp. oil over medium-high heat; saute eggplant and onion with salt and pepper until eggplant begins to soften, 4-5 minutes. Stir in the garlic; remove from heat.
2. Place naan on a baking sheet. Spread with ricotta cheese; sprinkle with oregano. Spread with the tomato sauce. Top with the eggplant mixture and whole basil leaves. Sprinkle with the mozzarella and Parmesan cheeses; drizzle with remaining oil. Bake until the crust is golden brown and the cheese is melted, 12-15 minutes. If desired, top with sliced basil.
TIP: Roasted garlic tomato sauce may be replaced with any flavored tomato sauce or a meatless pasta sauce.
½ PIZZA: 340 cal., 21g fat (7g sat. fat), 32mg chol., 996mg sod., 25g carb. (5g sugars, 3g fiber), 14g pro.

BUFFALO CHICKEN
BISCUITS

ORANGE DREAM PULL-APART BREAD

My baking therapy is to make treats for friends and co-workers. This pull-apart bread makes everyone smile as they face another busy day.
—*Vickie Friday Martin, Scroggins, TX*

- -

PREP: 25 min. • **BAKE:** 35 min.
MAKES: 10 servings

- 1 pkg. (8 oz.) cream cheese
- 2 tubes (7½ oz. each) small refrigerated buttermilk biscuits (10 count)
- 1 cup packed brown sugar
- 1 cup chopped pecans
- 4 tsp. grated orange zest
- ½ cup butter, melted

1. Preheat the oven to 375°. Cut the cream cheese into 20 pieces. Using a small knife, cut a horizontal pocket into the side of each biscuit; fill each with a piece of cream cheese. Pinch opening to seal.

2. In a shallow bowl, mix brown sugar, pecans and orange zest. Dip the biscuits in melted butter; roll in brown sugar mixture. Stand biscuits on their side in a greased 10-in. fluted tube pan.

3. Bake 35-40 minutes or until golden brown. Cool in pan 5 minutes before inverting onto a serving plate. Serve warm.

2 FILLED BISCUITS: 444 cal., 30g fat (12g sat. fat), 49mg chol., 612mg sod., 42g carb. (25g sugars, 1g fiber), 5g pro.

SICILIAN MEAT SAUCE

This ingredient list looks long, but most of the seasonings are already in your spice rack. Made in the slow cooker, it's so easy.
—*Emory Doty, Jasper, GA*

- -

PREP: 30 min. • **COOK:** 6 hours
MAKES: 12 servings

- 3 Tbsp. olive oil, divided
- 3 lbs. bone-in country-style pork ribs
- 1 medium onion, chopped
- 3 to 5 garlic cloves, minced
- 2 cans (28 oz. each) crushed or diced tomatoes, drained
- 1 can (14½ oz.) Italian diced tomatoes, drained
- 3 bay leaves
- 2 Tbsp. chopped fresh parsley
- 2 Tbsp. chopped capers, drained
- ½ tsp. dried basil
- ½ tsp. dried rosemary, crushed
- ½ tsp. dried thyme
- ½ tsp. crushed red pepper flakes
- ½ tsp. salt
- ½ tsp. sugar
- 1 cup beef broth
- ½ cup dry red wine or additional beef broth
  Hot cooked pasta
  Grated Parmesan cheese, optional

1. In a Dutch oven, heat 2 Tbsp. olive oil over medium-high heat. Brown pork ribs in batches; transfer to a 6-qt. slow cooker.

2. Add remaining oil to Dutch oven; saute onion for 2 minutes. Add the garlic; cook 1 minute more. Add next 11 ingredients. Pour in broth and red wine; bring to a light boil. Transfer to slow cooker. Cook, covered, about 6 hours or until pork is tender.

3. Discard bay leaves. Remove meat from slow cooker; shred or pull apart, discarding bones. Return meat to sauce. Serve over cooked pasta; if desired, sprinkle with Parmesan cheese.

1 CUP: 214 cal., 11g fat (3g sat. fat), 44mg chol., 822mg sod., 13g carb. (8g sugars, 3g fiber), 16g pro.

SICILIAN MEAT SAUCE

**PEPPERONI PIZZA
BAKED POTATOES**

PICKLED RAINBOW CHARD

Pickling adds pop to fresh foods, especially Swiss chard stems. In this easy refrigerator method, sweet meets tart and it all balances out overnight.
—Taste of Home *Test Kitchen*

- -

PREP: 10 min. • **COOK:** 5 min. + chilling
MAKES: 8 servings

2	bunches rainbow Swiss chard
1	small onion, halved and sliced
2	tsp. mixed pickling spices
½	tsp. celery seed
½	tsp. mustard seed
1	cup sugar
1	cup cider vinegar
⅓	cup water

1. Trim leaves from Swiss chard; save for another use. Cut stems into 2-in. pieces; place in a large heatproof nonreactive bowl. Add onion, pickling spices, celery seed and mustard seed.
2. In a small saucepan, combine the sugar, vinegar and water; bring to a boil. Cook 1 minute, stirring to dissolve sugar; pour carefully over chard mixture. Cool mixture completely. Refrigerate, covered, overnight, stirring occasionally.
1 SERVING: 48 cal., 0 fat (0 sat. fat), 0 chol., 211mg sod., 11g carb. (8g sugars, 2g fiber), 2g pro.

FAST FIX
PEPPERONI PIZZA BAKED POTATOES

These tasty taters were a spur-of-the-moment recipe I created from leftovers. It's truly a mash-up meal that combines two dinnertime favorites into one yummy, money-saving supper.
—*Dawn E. Lowenstein, Huntingdon Valley, PA*

- -

TAKES: 30 min. • **MAKES:** 4 servings

4	medium russet potatoes (about 8 oz each)
1	Tbsp. olive oil
1	cup sliced fresh mushrooms
1	small green pepper, chopped
1	small onion, chopped
1	garlic clove, minced
1	can (8 oz.) pizza sauce
⅓	cup mini sliced turkey pepperoni
½	cup shredded Italian cheese blend Fresh oregano leaves or dried oregano, optional

1. Preheat oven to 400°. Scrub potatoes; place on a microwave-safe plate. Pierce several times with a fork. Microwave the potatoes, uncovered, on high until tender, 12-15 minutes.
2. In a large skillet, heat oil over medium-high heat; saute mushrooms, pepper and onion until tender, 6-8 minutes. Add the garlic; cook and stir 1 minute. Stir in pizza sauce and pepperoni; heat through.
3. Place potatoes on a baking sheet; cut an "X" in the top of each. Fluff pulp with a fork. Top with vegetable mixture; sprinkle with cheese. Bake 5-7 minutes or until cheese is melted. If desired, sprinkle with oregano.
1 BAKED POTATO WITH TOPPINGS: 311 cal., 9g fat (3g sat. fat), 23mg chol., 515mg sod., 46g carb. (5g sugars, 6g fiber), 13g pro. **DIABETIC EXCHANGES:** 3 starch, 1 medium-fat meat, ½ fat.

CARAMEL APPLE
CUPCAKES

SWEETS ON THE CHEAP

Just because you're watching your budget doesn't mean you can't enjoy dessert!
From sweet snacks to decadent dinner finales, these tasty treats keep the
emphasis on flavor while cutting back on grocery bills. With more than a dozen
tooth-tingling bites to choose from, you'll always find the perfect nibble.

CARAMEL APPLE CUPCAKES

Bring these extra-special cupcakes to your next event and watch how quickly they disappear! With a caramel topping and spice-cake base, they're a delightful mix of two fall-favorite treats.

—Diane Halferty, Corpus Christi, TX

PREP: 25 min. • **BAKE:** 20 min. + cooling
MAKES: 1 dozen

- 1 pkg. spice or carrot cake mix (regular size)
- 2 cups chopped peeled tart apples (about 2 medium)
- 20 caramels
- 3 Tbsp. 2% milk
- 1 cup finely chopped pecans, toasted
- 12 wooden skewers (4½ in.)

1. Preheat oven to 350°. Line 12 jumbo muffin cups with paper liners.
2. Prepare cake mix batter according to the package directions; fold in apples. Fill the prepared cups three-fourths full. Bake until a toothpick inserted in center comes out clean, about 20 minutes. Cool 10 minutes before removing from pans; cool completely on a wire rack.
3. In a small saucepan, cook caramels and milk over low heat until smooth, stirring constantly. Spread over cupcakes. Sprinkle with pecans. Insert a wooden skewer in each.
NOTE: To toast nuts, bake in a shallow pan in a 350° oven for 5-10 minutes or cook in a skillet over low heat until lightly browned, stirring occasionally.
1 CUPCAKE: 365 cal., 19g fat (3g sat. fat), 48mg chol., 315mg sod., 48g carb. (30g sugars, 1g fiber), 5g pro.

MY TWO CENT$

"Instead of cupcakes, I made this in a 13x9-in. baking pan and served it to a group of medical students. There were no leftovers at the end of the evening! Instead of 20 caramels, I used a bag of caramel bits, and it worked just fine. I was rushed, and it saved me time to not have to unwrap the caramels. Will definitely make it again."

—GAPTOMOM, TASTEOFHOME.COM

PRETZEL GELATIN DESSERT

PRETZEL GELATIN DESSERT

This is one of my mother's absolute favorite desserts. The salty pretzel crust is the perfect complement to the sweet cream cheese filling.

—Erin Frakes, Moline, IL

PREP: 30 min. + chilling • **MAKES:** 12 servings

- 2 cups crushed pretzels
- ¾ cup butter, melted
- 2 Tbsp. sugar

FILLING

- 1 pkg. (8 oz.) cream cheese, softened
- 1 cup sugar
- 1 carton (8 oz.) frozen whipped topping, thawed

TOPPING

- 2 pkg. (3 oz. each) strawberry gelatin
- 2 cups boiling water
- ½ cup cold water
  Fresh strawberries and additional whipped topping, optional

1. Preheat oven to 350°. Mix crushed pretzels, butter and sugar; press onto bottom of an ungreased 13x9-in. baking dish. Bake 10 minutes. Cool completely.
2. For filling, beat cream cheese and sugar until smooth. Stir in whipped topping; spread over crust. Refrigerate, covered, until cold.
3. In a small bowl, dissolve gelatin in boiling water. Stir in cold water; refrigerate until partially set. Pour carefully over the filling. Refrigerate, covered, until firm, 4-6 hours.
4. Cut into squares. If desired, serve dessert with fresh strawberries and additional whipped topping.
1 PIECE: 401 cal., 22g fat (14g sat. fat), 50mg chol., 401mg sod., 48g carb. (37g sugars, 1g fiber), 4g pro.

ROOT BEER
FLOAT PIE

ROOT BEER FLOAT PIE

This is the kind of recipe your kids will look back on and always remember. And you don't even need to use an oven.

—*Cindy Reams, Philipsburg, PA*

- -

PREP: 15 min. + chilling • **MAKES:** 8 servings

- 1 carton (8 oz.) frozen reduced-fat whipped topping, thawed, divided
- ¾ cup cold diet root beer
- ½ cup fat-free milk
- 1 pkg. (1 oz.) sugar-free instant vanilla pudding mix
- 1 graham cracker crust (9 in.) Maraschino cherries, optional

1. Set aside and refrigerate ½ cup whipped topping for garnish. In a large bowl, whisk the root beer, milk and pudding mix for 2 minutes. Fold in half of the remaining whipped topping. Spread into graham cracker crust.

2. Spread remaining whipped topping over pie. Freeze for at least 8 hours or overnight.

3. Dollop reserved whipped topping over each serving; top with a maraschino cherry if desired.

1 SLICE: 185 cal., 8g fat (4g sat. fat), 0 chol., 275mg sod., 27g carb. (14g sugars, 0 fiber), 1g pro. **DIABETIC EXCHANGES:** 2 starch, 1 fat.

OUR TWO CENT$

If you are saving money by making your own graham cracker crust, try adding a dash or two of ground cinnamon to the sugar for an extra burst of flavor.

CEREAL & MILK ICE CREAM SANDWICHES

CEREAL & MILK ICE CREAM SANDWICHES

Use what's left at the bottom of your cereal boxes for these fun and frosty treats!

—Taste of Home *Test Kitchen*

- -

PREP: 10 min. + freezing • **MAKES:** 4 servings

- 2 Tbsp. Cap'n Crunch cereal
- 2 Tbsp. Froot Loops cereal
- 2 Tbsp. Fruity Pebbles cereal
- ¾ cup dulce de leche ice cream, softened
- 4 Rice Krispies treats (2.2 oz. each), halved lengthwise
- 1 Tbsp. hot caramel ice cream topping, warmed

In a shallow bowl, combine cereals. Spread ice cream onto the bottom half of each Rice Krispies treat. Drizzle with ice cream topping. Replace top half of Rice Krispies treat. Rolls sides in cereal mixture. Place on a baking sheet; freeze for at least 1 hour.

1 ICE CREAM SANDWICH: 381 cal., 9g fat (4g sat. fat), 38mg chol., 427mg sod., 70g carb. (30g sugars, 0 fiber), 5g pro.

AFTER-DINNER WHITE CHOCOLATE MOCHA

Here, a childhood favorite gets a grown-up makeover. If you're serving kids, just leave out the coffee granules.

—*Scarlett Elrod, Newnan, GA*

- -

TAKES: 15 min. • **MAKES:** 2 servings

- 1½ cups 2% milk
- 3 oz. white baking chocolate, chopped
- 2 Tbsp. instant coffee granules
- 1 tsp. vanilla extract Optional toppings: whipped cream and baking cocoa

1. In a small saucepan, heat milk over medium heat until bubbles form around sides of pan (do not boil).

2. Place the remaining ingredients in a blender. Add hot milk; cover and process until frothy. Serve in mugs. Top with whipped cream and cocoa if desired.

1 CUP: 342 cal., 19g fat (11g sat. fat), 23mg chol., 137mg sod., 34g carb. (33g sugars, 0 fiber), 9g pro.

APPLE DUMPLING BAKE

I received this recipe from a friend of mine, then tweaked it to suit my family's tastes. Mountain Dew is the secret ingredient in this rich apple dessert that's a snap to make.
—*Chris Shields, Monrovia, IN*

PREP: 15 min. • **BAKE:** 35 min.
MAKES: 8 servings

 2 medium Granny Smith apples
 2 tubes (8 oz. each) refrigerated
    crescent rolls
 1 cup sugar
 ⅓ cup butter, softened
 ½ tsp. ground cinnamon
 ¾ cup Mountain Dew soda
    Vanilla ice cream

1. Preheat oven to 350°. Peel, core and cut each apple into eight wedges. Unroll both tubes of crescent dough; separate each into eight triangles. Wrap a triangle around each wedge, pinching edges to seal. Place in a greased 13x9-in. baking dish.

2. In a bowl, mix sugar, butter and cinnamon until blended; sprinkle over the dumplings. Slowly pour Mountain Dew around the rolls (do not stir).

3. Bake, uncovered, until golden brown and apples are tender, 35-40 minutes. Serve warm with ice cream.

2 DUMPLINGS: 414 cal., 20g fat (9g sat. fat), 20mg chol., 510mg sod., 55g carb. (35g sugars, 1g fiber), 4g pro.

FLOURLESS DARK CHOCOLATE CAKE

MARIE PARKER
Milwaukee, WI

FLOURLESS DARK CHOCOLATE CAKE

Here's a simple cake that's rich, elegant and easy on the pocketbook. For a finishing touch, top with powdered sugar, cocoa or liqueur-flavored whipped cream.
—*Marie Parker, Milwaukee, WI*

PREP: 25 min. • **BAKE:** 30 min. + cooling
MAKES: 12 servings

 4   large eggs, separated
 3   Tbsp. butter
 8   oz. dark baking chocolate, chopped
 ⅓ cup plus ¼ cup sugar, divided
 1   container (2½ oz.) prune baby food
 1½ tsp. vanilla extract
     Confectioners' sugar

1. Place egg whites in a small bowl; let stand at room temperature 30 minutes. Preheat oven to 350°. Coat a 9-in. springform pan with cooking spray; place on a baking sheet.

2. In a small saucepan, melt the butter and chocolate over low heat, stirring constantly. Remove from heat; cool slightly. In a large bowl, beat egg yolks on high speed 3 minutes or until slightly thickened. Gradually add ⅓ cup sugar, beating mixture until thick and lemon-colored. Beat in baby food, vanilla and the chocolate mixture.

3. With clean beaters, beat egg whites on medium until soft peaks form. Gradually add remaining sugar, 1 Tbsp. at a time, beating on high after each addition until the sugar is dissolved. Continue beating until stiff glossy peaks form. Fold a fourth of the egg whites into the chocolate mixture, then fold in the remaining whites.

4. Pour into the prepared pan. Bake until a toothpick inserted in center comes out with moist crumbs, 30-35 minutes. Cool on a wire rack 20 minutes. Loosen sides from pan with a knife; remove rim from pan. Cool the cake completely. Dust with confectioners' sugar before serving.

1 SLICE: 188 cal., 11g fat (6g sat. fat), 78mg chol., 50mg sod., 22g carb. (18g sugars, 2g fiber), 4g pro.

RHUBARB MALLOW COBBLER

My mom used to make this when I was growing up. Now we take fresh rhubarb to my son in Texas so he can share this treat with his family.

—*Judy Kay Warwick, Webster City, IA*

- -

PREP: 15 min. • **BAKE:** 40 min.
MAKES: 12 servings

4	cups diced fresh or frozen rhubarb
2½	cups sugar, divided
1	cup miniature marshmallows
½	cup butter, softened
1	tsp. vanilla extract
1¾	cups all-purpose flour
3	tsp. baking powder
½	tsp. salt
½	cup whole milk

1. In a large bowl, combine the rhubarb and 1½ cups sugar. Transfer to a greased 11x7-in. baking dish. Sprinkle with marshmallows.
2. In a small bowl, cream the butter, vanilla and remaining sugar until light and fluffy. Combine the flour, baking powder and salt; add to creamed mixture alternately with milk. Beat just until moistened; spoon over diced rhubarb.
3. Bake at 350° until topping is golden brown, 40-45 minutes. Serve warm.
NOTE: If using frozen rhubarb, measure rhubarb while still frozen, then thaw completely. Drain in a colander, but do not press liquid out.
1 SERVING: 323 cal., 8g fat (5g sat. fat), 22mg chol., 285mg sod., 61g carb. (45g sugars, 1g fiber), 3g pro.

SNICKERDOODLES

The history of these whimsically named treats is widely disputed. Their popularity, however, is undeniable. Help yourself to one of our soft cinnamon-sugared cookies and see for yourself.

—*Taste of Home Test Kitchen*

- -

PREP: 20 min. • **BAKE:** 10 min./batch
MAKES: 2½ dozen

½	cup butter, softened
1	cup plus 2 Tbsp. sugar, divided
1	large egg
½	tsp. vanilla extract
1½	cups all-purpose flour
¼	tsp. baking soda
¼	tsp. cream of tartar
1	tsp. ground cinnamon

1. Preheat oven to 375°. Cream butter and 1 cup sugar until light and fluffy; beat in egg and vanilla. In another bowl, whisk together the flour, baking soda and cream of tartar; gradually beat into the creamed mixture.
2. In a small bowl, mix cinnamon and the remaining sugar. Shape dough into 1-in. balls; roll in cinnamon sugar. Place 2 in. apart on ungreased baking sheets.
3. Bake until light brown, 10-12 minutes. Remove from pans to wire racks to cool.
1 COOKIE: 81 cal., 3g fat (2g sat. fat), 15mg chol., 44mg sod., 12g carb. (7g sugars, 0 fiber), 1g pro.

RHUBARB MALLOW COBBLER

FIRST-PLACE COCONUT MACAROONS

FAST FIX | 5 INGREDIENTS
LEMON MERINGUE FLOATS

I dreamed of this float idea one night and woke up knowing I needed to make it. Thank you, Mr. Sandman!
—*Cindy Reams, Philipsburg, PA*

- -

TAKES: 5 min. • **MAKES:** 6 servings

- 3 cups vanilla ice cream, softened if necessary
- 18 miniature meringue cookies
- 6 cups cold pink lemonade

Place ½ cup ice cream and three cookies in each of six tall glasses. Top with lemonade. Serve immediately.
1½ CUPS WITH 3 COOKIES: 282 cal., 7g fat (4g sat. fat), 29mg chol., 77mg sod., 51g carb. (48g sugars, 0 fiber), 3g pro.
HEALTH TIP: Make your floats with frozen yogurt for a slimmed-down treat.

YUMMY COOKIE BARS

I received the recipe for these treats from a co-worker, and they're always a success when I make them. I find the bars cut more easily if you make them a day in advance and refrigerate them overnight.
—*Teresa Hamman, Slayton, MN*

- -

PREP: 20 min. • **BAKE:** 25 min. + cooling
MAKES: 2 dozen

- 1 pkg. white cake mix (regular size)
- ½ cup canola oil
- 2 large eggs
- ½ cup butter, cubed
- ½ cup milk chocolate chips
- ½ cup peanut butter chips
- 1 can (14 oz.) sweetened condensed milk

1. Preheat oven to 350°. In a large bowl, combine cake mix, oil and eggs. Press half of dough into a greased 13x9-in. baking pan.
2. In a small microwave-safe bowl, melt butter and chips; stir until smooth. Stir in milk. Pour over crust. Drop remaining dough by teaspoonfuls over the top.
3. Bake until the edges are golden brown, 25-30 minutes. Cool completely on a wire rack before cutting into bars.
1 BAR: 261 cal., 14g fat (5g sat. fat), 34mg chol., 211mg sod., 30g carb. (22g sugars, 0 fiber), 4g pro.

5 INGREDIENTS
FIRST-PLACE COCONUT MACAROONS

These cookies earned me a first-place ribbon at the county fair. When I make them to give away, my husband always asks me where ours are! I especially like the fact that the recipe makes a small enough batch for just the two of us to nibble on.
—*Penny Ann Habeck, Shawano, WI*

- -

PREP: 10 min. • **BAKE:** 20 min./batch
MAKES: about 1½ dozen

- 1⅓ cups sweetened shredded coconut
- ⅓ cup sugar
- 2 Tbsp. all-purpose flour
- ⅛ tsp. salt
- 2 large egg whites
- ½ tsp. vanilla extract

1. In a small bowl, combine the coconut, sugar, flour and salt. Add egg whites and vanilla; mix well.
2. Drop by rounded teaspoonfuls onto greased baking sheets. Bake at 325° for 18-20 minutes or until golden brown. Cool on a wire rack.
1 COOKIE: 54 cal., 2g fat (2g sat. fat), 0 chol., 41mg sod., 8g carb. (7g sugars, 0 fiber), 1g pro. **DIABETIC EXCHANGES:** ½ starch, ½ fat.

CINDY REAMS
Phillpsburg, PA

LEMON MERINGUE FLOATS

PEACH COBBLER DUMP CAKE

This recipe has the best of both worlds: a sweet, tender cake and a beautifully crisp cobbler topping. Add a scoop of vanilla ice cream on the side, and dessert's golden.
—*Keri Sparks, Little Elm, TX*

PREP: 10 min. • **BAKE:** 35 min.
MAKES: 15 servings

2   cans (15 oz. each) sliced peaches in extra-light syrup
2   Tbsp. brown sugar
1   tsp. ground cinnamon
1   pkg. yellow cake mix (regular size)
¾ cup sliced almonds
½ cup cold butter

1. Preheat oven to 350°. Pour one can of peaches into a greased 13x9-in. baking dish. Drain remaining can of peaches and add to baking dish; sprinkle with the brown sugar and cinnamon. Sprinkle with cake mix and sliced almonds.
2. Cut butter into very thin slices; arrange over top, spacing evenly. Bake until golden brown and fruit is bubbly, 35-40 minutes. Serve warm.
1 SERVING: 234 cal., 11g fat (5g sat. fat), 16mg chol., 242mg sod., 34g carb. (22g sugars, 1g fiber), 2g pro.

5 INGREDIENTS

FROZEN BERRY & YOGURT SWIRLS

I enjoy these frozen yogurt pops because they double as a healthy snack and a cool, creamy sweet treat.
—*Colleen Ludovice, Wauwatosa, WI*

PREP: 15 min. + freezing • **MAKES:** 10 pops

10 plastic or paper cups (3 oz. each)
2¾ cups fat-free honey Greek yogurt
1   cup mixed fresh berries
¼ cup water
2   Tbsp. sugar
10 wooden pop sticks

1. Fill each cup with about ¼ cup yogurt. Place berries, water and sugar in a food processor; pulse until berries are finely chopped. Spoon 1½ Tbsp. berry mixture into each cup. Stir gently with a pop stick to swirl.
2. Top cups with foil; insert pop sticks through foil. Freeze until firm.
1 POP: 60 cal., 0 fat (0 sat. fat), 0 chol., 28mg sod., 9g carb. (8g sugars, 1g fiber), 6g pro.
DIABETIC EXCHANGES: 1 starch.
FOR FROZEN CLEMENTINE & YOGURT SWIRLS: Substitute 1 cup seeded clementine segments (about five medium) and ¼ cup orange juice for berries, water and sugar; proceed as directed.

PEACH COBBLER DUMP CAKE

S'MORES CRESCENT ROLLS

CHOCOLATE CHIP CREAM CHEESE BARS

Lower in fat and calories than you might guess, these bars boast a great chocolaty flavor. They make a fun contribution to parties and potlucks.
—*Jennifer Rafferty, Milford, OH*

PREP: 15 min. • **BAKE:** 20 min. + cooling
MAKES: 2 dozen

- 1 pkg. German chocolate cake mix (regular size)
- ⅓ cup canola oil
- 1 large egg

FILLING
- 1 pkg. (8 oz.) reduced-fat cream cheese
- ⅓ cup sugar
- 1 large egg, lightly beaten
- 1 cup miniature semisweet chocolate chips

1. Preheat oven to 350°. Combine the cake mix, oil and egg; mix until blended. Reserve 1 cup cake mixture for topping. Press the remaining mixture into a 13x9-in. baking pan coated with cooking spray. Bake until set, 10-12 minutes.
2. For filling, beat cream cheese and sugar until smooth. Beat in egg. Spread over crust. Sprinkle with chocolate chips and reserved cake mixture.
3. Bake until set, 18-20 minutes. Cool on a wire rack. Cut into bars. Store in refrigerator.
1 BAR: 187 cal., 9g fat (3g sat. fat), 24mg chol., 207mg sod., 25g carb. (18g sugars, 0 fiber), 3g pro. **DIABETIC EXCHANGES:** 1½ starch, 1½ fat.

FAST FIX | 5 INGREDIENTS
S'MORES CRESCENT ROLLS

Here's how to score indoor s'mores: Grab crescent dough and Nutella. Invite the kids to help with this rolled-up version of the campfire classic.
—*Cathy Trochelman, Brookfield, WI*

- -

TAKES: 25 min. • **MAKES:** 8 servings

- 1 tube (8 oz.) refrigerated crescent rolls
- ¼ cup Nutella, divided
- 2 whole graham crackers, broken up
- 2 Tbsp. milk chocolate chips
- ⅔ cup miniature marshmallows

1. Preheat oven to 375°. Unroll crescent dough; separate into eight triangles. Place 1 tsp. Nutella at the wide end of each dough triangle; sprinkle with the graham crackers, chocolate chips and marshmallows. Roll up and place on ungreased baking sheets, point side down; curve to form crescents. Bake until golden brown, 9-11 minutes.

2. In a microwave, warm remaining Nutella to reach a drizzling consistency; spoon over rolls. Serve warm.
1 ROLL: 201 cal., 10g fat (3g sat. fat), 1mg chol., 256mg sod., 25g carb. (12g sugars, 1g fiber), 3g pro.

OUR TWO CENT$
Get creative with s'mores crescent rolls. Try adding a drizzle of caramel ice cream topping over the tops or replace the milk chocolate chips with butterscotch chips. You can even stuff each roll with a few raspberries if you'd like.

RECIPE INDEX